Fish Dish

Publisher & Creative Director: Nick Wells
Senior Editor: Cat Emslie
Designer: Theresa Maynard
With thanks to: Gina Steer, Victoria Lyle,
Lauren Perazza–Fontanez and Julie Pallot

This is a **FLAME TREE** Book

FLAME TREE PUBLISHING
Crabtree Hall, Crabtree Lane
Fulham, London SW6 6TY
United Kingdom
www.flametreepublishing.com

Flame Tree is part of The Foundry Creative Media Company Limited

First published 2008

10 12 11 09

5 7 9 10 8 6 4

ISBN: 978-1-84786-181-8

A copy of the CIP data for this book is available from the British Library.

Printed in China

Fish Dishes

Quick and Easy, Proven Recipes

**FLAME TREE
PUBLISHING**

Contents

Contents

Pasta, Rice & Potatoes

Baked, Grilled, Seared, Steamed & Poached **200**

Contents

Curries, Stews & Stir-fries **268**

Deep-fried, Pies & Pastry

Hygiene in the Kitchen

It is well worth remembering that many foods can carry some form of bacteria. In most cases, the worst it will lead to is a bout of food poisoning or gastroenteritis, although for certain groups this can be more serious. The risk can be reduced or eliminated by good food hygiene and proper cooking.

Do not buy food that is past its sell-by date and do not consume any food that is past its use-by date. When buying food, use the eyes and nose. If the food looks tired, limp or a bad colour or it has a rank, acrid or simply bad smell, do not buy or eat it under any circumstances.

Regularly clean, defrost and clear out the refrigerator or freezer – it is worth checking the packaging to see exactly how long each product is safe to freeze.

Dish cloths and tea towels must be washed and changed regularly. Ideally use disposable cloths which should be replaced on a daily basis. More durable cloths should be left

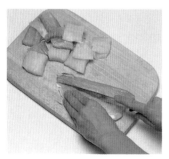

to soak in bleach, then washed in the washing machine on a boil wash.

Always keep your hands, cooking utensils and food preparation surfaces clean and never allow pets to climb on to any work surfaces.

Buying

Avoid bulk buying where possible, especially fresh produce such as meat, poultry, fish, fruit and vegetables unless buying for the freezer. Fresh foods lose their nutritional value rapidly so buying a little at a time minimises loss of nutrients. It also eliminates a packed refrigerator which reduces the effectiveness of the refrigeration process.

When buying frozen foods, ensure that they are not heavily iced on the outside. Place in the freezer as soon as possible after purchase.

Preparation

Make sure that all work surfaces and utensils are clean and dry. Separate chopping boards should be used for raw and cooked meats, fish and vegetables. It is worth washing all fruits and vegetables regardless of whether they are going to be eaten raw or lightly cooked. Do not reheat food more than once.

All poultry must be thoroughly thawed before cooking. Leave the food in the refrigerator until it is completely thawed. Once defrosted, the chicken should be cooked as soon as possible. The only time food can be refrozen is when the food has been thoroughly thawed then cooked. Once the food has cooled then it can be frozen again for one month.

All poultry and game (except for duck) must be cooked thoroughly. When cooked the juices will run clear. Other

meats, like minced meat and pork should be cooked right the way through. Fish should turn opaque, be firm in texture and break easily into large flakes.

Storing, Refrigerating and Freezing

Meat, poultry, fish, seafood and dairy products should all be refrigerated. The temperature of the refrigerator should be between 1–5°C/34–41°F while the freezer temperature should not rise above -18°C/-0.4°F. When refrigerating cooked food, allow it to cool down quickly and completely before refrigerating. Hot food will raise the temperature of the refrigerator and possibly affect or spoil other food stored in it.

Food within the refrigerator and freezer should always be covered. Raw and cooked food should be stored in separate parts of the refrigerator. Cooked food should be kept on the top shelves of the refrigerator, while raw meat, poultry and fish should be placed on bottom shelves to avoid drips and cross-contamination.

High-Risk Foods

Certain foods may carry risks to people who are considered vulnerable such as the elderly, the ill, pregnant women, babies and those suffering from a recurring illness. It is advisable to avoid those foods which belong to a higher-risk category.

There is a slight chance that some eggs carry the bacteria salmonella. Cook the eggs until both the yolk and the white are firm to eliminate this risk. Sauces including Hollandaise, mayonnaise, mousses, soufflés and meringues all use raw or lightly cooked eggs, as do custard-based dishes, ice creams and sorbets. These are all considered high-risk foods to the vulnerable groups mentioned above. Certain meats and poultry also carry the potential risk of salmonella and so should be cooked thoroughly until the juices run clear and there is no pinkness left. Unpasteurised products such as milk, cheese (especially soft cheese), pâté, meat (both raw and cooked) all have the potential risk of listeria and should be avoided.

When buying seafood, buy from a reputable source. Fish should have bright clear eyes, shiny skin and bright pink or red gills. The fish should feel stiff to the touch, with a slight smell of sea air and iodine. The flesh of fish steaks and fillets should be translucent with no signs of discolouration. Avoid any molluscs that are open or do not close when tapped lightly. Univalves such as cockles or winkles should withdraw into their shells when lightly prodded. Squid and octopus should have firm flesh and a pleasant sea smell.

Care is required when freezing seafood. It is imperative to check whether the fish has been frozen before. If it has been, then it should not be frozen again under any circumstances.

Nutrition
The Role of Essential Nutrients

A healthy and well-balanced diet is the body's primary energy source. In children, it constitutes the building blocks for future health as well as providing lots of energy. In adults, it encourages self-healing and regeneration within the body. A well-balanced diet will provide the body with all the essential nutrients it needs. This can be achieved by eating a variety of foods, demonstrated in the pyramid below:

Fats
milk, yoghurt
and cheese

Proteins
meat, fish, poultry, eggs,
nuts and pulses

Fruits and Vegetables

Starchy Carbohydrates
cereals, potatoes, bread, rice and pasta

Fats

Fats fall into two categories: saturated and unsaturated fats. It is very important that a healthy balance is achieved within the diet. Fats are an essential part of the diet and a source of energy and provide essential fatty acids and fat soluble vitamins. The right balance of fats should boost the body's immunity to infection and keep muscles, nerves and arteries in good condition. Saturated fats are of animal origin and are hard when stored at room temperature. They can be found in dairy produce, meat, eggs, margarines and hard white cooking fat (lard) as well as in manufactured products such as pies, biscuits and cakes. A high intake of saturated fat over many years has been proven to increase heart disease and high blood cholesterol levels and often leads to weight gain. The aim of a healthy diet is to keep the fat content low in the foods that we eat. Lowering the amount of saturated fat that we consume is very important, but this does not mean that it is good to consume lots of other types of fat.

There are two kinds of unsaturated fats: polyunsaturated and monounsaturated. Polyunsaturated fats include the following oils: safflower oil, soybean oil, corn oil and sesame oil. Within the polyunsaturated group are Omega oils. The Omega-3 oils are of significant interest because they have been found to be particularly beneficial to coronary health and can encourage brain growth and development. The oils are derived from oily fish such as salmon, mackerel, herring, pilchards and sardines. It is recommended that we should eat these types of fish at least once a week. However, for those who do not eat fish, liver oil supplements are available in most supermarkets and health shops. It is suggested that these supplements should be taken on a daily basis. The most popular oils that are high in monounsaturates are olive oil, sunflower oil and peanut oil. The Mediterranean diet which is based on a diet high in monounsaturated fats is recommended for heart health. Also, monounsaturated fats are known to help reduce the levels of LDL (the bad) cholestrol. However, one type of unsaturated fat which should be avoided at all costs is 'trans fat'. This can be poly- or monounsaturated and is most commonly found in processed foods containing 'hydrogenated' oil or fat.

Proteins

Composed of amino acids, proteins perform a wide variety of essential functions for the body including supplying energy and building and repairing tissues. Good sources of proteins are eggs, milk, yoghurt, cheese, meat, fish, poultry, eggs, nuts and pulses (see the second level of the pyramid). Some of these foods, however, contain saturated fats. To strike a nutritional balance eat generous amounts of vegetable protein foods such as soya, beans, lentils, peas and nuts.

Fruits and Vegetables

Not only are fruits and vegetables the most visually appealing foods, but they are extremely good for us, providing essential vitamins and minerals essential for growth, repair and protection in the human body. Fruits and vegetables are low in calories and are responsible for regulating the body's metabolic processes and controlling the composition of its fluids and cells.

Minerals

CALCIUM Important for healthy bones and teeth, nerve transmission, muscle contraction, blood clotting and hormone function. Calcium promotes a healthy heart, improves skin, relieves aching muscles and bones, maintains the correct acid-alkaline balance and reduces menstrual cramps. Good sources are dairy products, small bones of small fish, nuts, pulses, fortified white flours, breads and green leafy vegetables.

CHROMIUM Part of the glucose tolerance factor, chromium balances blood sugar levels, helps to normalise hunger and reduce cravings, improves lifespan, helps protect DNA and is essential for heart function. Good sources are brewer's yeast, wholemeal bread, rye bread, oysters, potatoes, green peppers, butter and parsnips.

IODINE Important for the manufacture of thyroid hormones and for normal development. Good sources of iodine are seafood, seaweed, milk and dairy products.

IRON As a component of haemoglobin, iron carries oxygen around the body. It is vital for normal growth and development. Good sources are liver, corned beef, red meat, fortified breakfast cereals, pulses, green leafy vegetables, egg yolk and cocoa and cocoa products.

MAGNESIUM Important for efficient functioning of metabolic enzymes and development of the skeleton. Magnesium promotes healthy muscles by helping them to relax and is therefore good for PMS. It is also important for heart muscles and the nervous system. Good sources are nuts, green vegetables, meat, cereals, milk and yoghurt.

PHOSPHORUS Forms and maintains bones and teeth, builds muscle tissue, helps maintain pH of the body, aids metabolism and energy production. Phosphorus is present in almost all foods.

POTASSIUM Enables nutrients to move into cells, while waste products move out; promotes healthy nerves and muscles; maintains fluid balance in the body; helps secretion of insulin for blood sugar control to produce constant energy; relaxes muscles; maintains heart functioning and stimulates gut movement to encourage proper elimination. Good sources are fruit, vegetables, milk and bread.

SELENIUM Antioxidant properties help to protect against free radicals and carcinogens. Selenium reduces inflammation, stimulates the immune system to fight infections, promotes a healthy heart and helps vitamin E's action. It is also required for the male reproductive system and is needed for metabolism. Good sources are tuna, liver, kidney, meat, eggs, cereals, nuts and dairy products.

SODIUM Important in helping to control body fluid and balance, preventing dehydration. Sodium is involved in muscle and nerve function and helps move nutrients into cells. All foods are good sources; however, processed, pickled and salted foods can contain too much sodium.

ZINC Important for metabolism and the healing of wounds.

It also aids ability to cope with stress, promotes a healthy nervous system and brain especially in the growing foetus, aids bones and teeth formation and is essential for constant energy. Good sources are liver, meat, pulses, whole-grain cereals, nuts and oysters.

Vitamins

VITAMIN A Important for cell growth and developmemt and for the formation of visual pigments in the eye. Vitamin A comes in two forms: retinol and beta-carotenes. Retinol is found in liver, meat and meat products and whole milk and its products. Beta-carotene is a powerul antioxidant and is found in red and yellow fruits and vegetables such as carrots, mangoes and apricots.

VITAMIN B1 Important in releasing energy from carboydrate-containing foods. Good sources are yeast and yeast products, bread, fortified breakfast cereals and potatoes.

VITAMIN B2 Important for metabolism of proteins, fats and carbohydrates to produce energy. Good sources are meat, yeast extracts, fortified breakfast cereals and milk and its products.

VITAMIN B3 Required for metabolism of food into energy production. Good sources are milk and milk products, fortified breakfast cereals, pulses, meat, poultry and eggs.

VITAMIN B5 Important for metabolism of food and energy production. All foods are good sources but especially fortified breakfast cereals, whole-grain bread and dairy products.

VITAMIN B6 Important for metabolism of protein and fat. It may also be involved with the regulation of sex hormones. Good sources are liver, fish, pork, soya beans and peanuts.

VITAMIN B12 Important for the production of red blood cells and DNA. It is vital for growth and the nervous system. Good sources are meat, fish, eggs, poultry and milk.

BIOTIN Important for metabolism of fatty acids. Good sources of biotin are liver, kidney, eggs and nuts. Micro-organisms also manufacture this vitamin in the gut.

VITAMIN C Important for healing wounds and the formation of collagen which keeps skin and bones strong. It is an important antioxidant. Good sources are fruits, soft summer fruits and vegetables.

VITAMIN D Important for absorption and handling of calcium to help build bone strength. Good sources are oily fish, eggs, whole milk and milk products, margarine and, of course, sufficient exposure to sunlight, as vitamin D is made in the skin.

VITAMIN E Important as an antioxidant vitamin helping to protect cell membranes from damage. Good sources are vegetable oils, margarines, seeds, nuts and green vegetables.

FOLIC ACID Critical during pregnancy for the development of the brain and nerves. It is always essential for brain and nerve function and is needed for utilising protein and red blood cell formation. Good sources are whole-grain cereals, fortified breakfast cereals, green leafy vegetables, oranges and liver.

VITAMIN K Important for controlling blood clotting. Good sources are cauliflower, Brussels sprouts, lettuce, cabbage, beans, broccoli, peas, asparagus, potatoes, corn oil, tomatoes and milk.

Carbohydrates

Carbohydrates are an energy source and come in two forms: starch and sugar. Starch carbohydrates are also known as complex carbohydrates and they include all cereals, potatoes, breads, rice and pasta (see the fourth level of the pyramid). Eating wholegrain varieties of these foods also provides fibre. Diets high in fibre are believed to be beneficial in helping to prevent bowel cancer and can also keep cholesterol down. High-fibre diets are also good for those concerned about weight gain. Fibre is bulky and fills the stomach, therefore reducing hunger pangs. Sugar carbohydrates, which are also known as fast-release carbohydrates because of the quick fix of energy they give to the body, include sugar and sugar-sweetened products such as jams and syrups. Milk provides lactose which is a milk sugar and fruits provide fructose which is a fruit sugar.

Preparing & Cooking Fish & Seafood

Requiring only minimal cooking, all fish is an excellent choice for speedy and nutritious meals. There are two categories of fish: white and oily (see pages 18–19). Seafood can be divided into three categories: shellfish, crustaceans and molluscs (see page 20).

Both types of fish are sold fresh or frozen as small whole fish, fillets or cutlets. Store as soon as possible in the refrigerator. Remove from the wrappings, place on a plate, cover lightly and store towards the top. Use within one day of purchase. If using frozen, thaw slowly in the refrigerator and use within one day of thawing.

Seafood should be eaten as fresh as possible. Live seafood gives the best flavour, as long as it is consumed on the day of purchase. If live is not available, buy from a reputable source and eat on the day of purchase, refrigerating until required. Clean all seafood thoroughly and with mussels and clams, discard any that do not close when tapped lightly before cooking. After cooking, discard any that have not opened.

Cleaning Fish

When cleaning whole fish, first remove the scales. Using a round bladed knife, gently scrape the knife along the fish starting from the tail towards the head. Rinse frequently. To clean round fish, make a slit along the abdomen from

the gills to the tail using a small, sharp knife and scrape out the innards. Rinse thoroughly.

For flat fish, open the cavity under the gills and remove the innards. Rinse. Remove the gills and fins and, if preferred, the tail and head. Rinse thoroughly in cold water and pat dry. Cutlet and fillets simply need lightly rinsing in cold water and patting dry.

Skinning Fish

For whole flat fish, clean and remove the fins as before. Make a small cut on the dark side of the fish across the tail and slip your thumb between the skin and flesh. Loosen the skin along the side. Holding the fish firmly with one hand, rip the skin off with the other. The white skin can be removed in the same way.

Round fish are normally cooked with the skin on, but if you do wish to skin them, start from the head and cut a narrow strip of skin along the backbone. Cut below the head and loosen the skin with the point of the knife. Dip your fingers in salt for a better grip and gently pull the skin down towards the tail. Take care not to break the flesh.

Filleting Fish

To fillet flat fish, use a sharp knife and make a cut along the line of bones. Insert the knife under the flesh and carefully cut it with long sweeping strokes. Cut the first fillet from the left-hand side, working from head to tail. Turn the fish round and repeat, this time cutting from tail to head. Turn the fish over and repeat on this side.

For round fish, cut along the centre of the back to the bone and then cut along the abdomen. Cleanly remove the flesh with short, sharp strokes from the head downwards pressing the knife against the bones. Turn the fish over and repeat. This is suitable for larger fish such as salmon.

To fillet herring and mackerel, discard the head, tail and fins and clean, reserving any roe if applicable. Place on a chopping board and gently press along the backbone to open fully and loosen the bone. Turn the fish over, ease the backbone up and remove, taking as many of the small bones as possible at the same time.

Basic Fish Recipes
Poached Fish

Clean the fish, remove scales if necessary and rinse thoroughly. Place in a large frying pan with 1 small peeled and sliced onion and carrot, 1 bay leaf, 5 peppercorns and a few parsley stalks. Pour over sufficient cold water to barely cover, then bring to the boil over a medium heat. Reduce the heat to a simmer, cover and cook gently for 8–10 minutes for fillets and 10–15 minutes for whole fish.

This method is suitable for fillets and small whole fish. When the fish is cooked, the flesh should yield easily when pierced with a round bladed knife, and the fish should look opaque.

Grilled Fish

Line a grill rack with tin foil and preheat the grill to medium high just before grilling. Lightly rinse the fish, pat it dry and place on the foil-lined grill rack. Season with salt and pepper and brush lightly with a little oil. Cook under the grill for 8–10 minutes or until cooked, turning the heat down if the fish is cooking too quickly. Sprinkle with herbs or pour over a little melted butter or herb-flavoured olive oil to serve.

This method is suitable for fresh fish fillets (not smoked), sardines and other small whole fish. Make 3 slashes across whole fish before grilling.

Griddled Fish

Rinse the fish fillet, pat dry and, if desired, marinate in a marinade of your choice for 30 minutes. Heat a griddle pan until smoking and add the fish, skin side down. Cook for 5 minutes, pressing the fish down with a fish slice. Turn the fish over and continue to cook for a further 4–5 minutes or until cooked to personal preference.

Types of Fish & Seafood

White Fish

White fish such as cod, haddock, plaice or coley are an excellent source of protein and have a low fat content. They also contain vitamin B12 and niacin, plus important minerals such as phosphorous, iodine, selenium and potassium.

BASS Sea fish. Suitable for grilling or frying. Large bass can be poached whole. Has very white flesh. At its best from May to August.

SEA BREAM Sea fish. Suitable for grilling, poaching and frying, can also be stuffed and baked or poached. Has white, firm flesh with a delicate flavour. At its best from June to December.

BRILL Sea fish. Suitable for grilling, baking or poaching and serving cold. Has firm flesh with a slight yellow tinge. At its best from April to August, but available all year.

COD Sea fish. Also available smoked. Suitable for all types of cooking. Perhaps the most popular and versatile of all fish, with white flesh and a very delicate flavour. At its best from October to May but available all year round.

COLEY Sea fish. Suitable for all types of cooking. One of the cheaper varieties of fish. Has a greyish-coloured flesh which turns slightly white on cooking. Available all year round.

HADDOCK Sea fish. Also available smoked. Suitable for all types of cooking. Has a firm, white flesh with a slightly stronger flavour than cod. At its best from September to February, but available all year round.

HAKE Sea fish. Suitable for all methods of cooking. Has a firm, close-textured white flesh and is considered to have a better flavour than cod. At its best from June to January, but available all year round.

HALIBUT Sea fish. Suitable for all methods of cooking except deep frying. A large flat fish with excellent flavour. At its best from August to April but available all year round.

JOHN DORY Sea fish. Suitable for poaching or baking whole, or fillets can be cooked as for sole. Has a firm, white flesh with good flavour. Can be difficult to find. At its best from October to December.

MONKFISH Sea fish. Suitable for all methods of cooking including roasting. A firm, white fish with 'meaty' texture. A good substitute for lobster. Only the tail is eaten – the central bone is normally discarded and the two fillets are used. Available all year round.

PLAICE Sea fish. The whole fish is suitable for grilling and pan frying, whilst fillets can be steamed, stuffed and rolled or

used as goujons. A flat fish with distinctive dark grey/black skin with red spots. Has soft, white flesh with a very delicate flavour. Available all year round.

RED MULLET Sea fish. Suitable for grilling, frying or baking. Has a firm, white flesh and red skin. At its best from May to September.

SKATE Sea fish. Suitable for grilling, frying or poaching. Only the wings are eaten and the bones are soft and gelatinous. A white fish with a delicate flavour. At its best from September to April.

SOLE Sea fish. Suitable for frying or grilling. Has a firm, yet delicate white skin with a delicious flavour. Available all year round. Dover sole is recognised by its dark grey/black skin and is considered by many to be the finest of the sole varieties. Lemon sole, which is more pointed, Witch and Torbay soles have the same qualities but the flavour is not as good.

TURBOT Sea fish. Suitable for grilling or baking. Normally sold in cutlets, it has a creamy, white flesh with a delicious flavour which is reputed to be the best of all flat fish. At its best from March to August.

WHITING Sea fish. Suitable for all methods of cooking. Cooked whole or in fillets, it has a white, delicately-flavoured flesh. Available all year round.

Oily Fish

Oily fish such as sardines, mackerel, salmon and herring have a higher fat content than white fish but are an excellent source of Omega-3 polyunsaturated fatty acids, important in fighting heart disease, cancers and arthritis. Oily fish also contain niacin, B6, B12 and D vitamins and selenium, iodine, potassium and phosphorous minerals. The flavour is stronger and more robust, enabling stronger flavours such as chilli and garlic to be used. It is recommended that at least one portion of oily fish should be eaten each week.

HERRING Sea fish. Suitable for frying, grilling or preserving in vinegar to make rollmops. A small fish with creamy-coloured flesh and fairly strong flavour, herring contain many bones. At its best from June to December

MACKEREL Sea fish. Suitable for grilling and frying, whilst whole fish can be stuffed or baked. Have a distinctive bluish-coloured skin with blue/black lines and a creamy underside. At its best from April to June.

PILCHARD Sea fish. Normally sold canned but fresh pilchards are sometimes available. Similar to herring but smaller. Caught off the Cornish coast all year round.

SALMON Freshwater fish. The whole fish is suitable for poaching or baking to serve hot or cold. Fillets or cutlets can be fried, grilled, baked, steamed or barbecued. Farmed salmon has a milder flavour than wild, and the deep pink flesh is not as firm as that of wild salmon. The smaller wild salmon is much paler in colour, with a far-superior flavour and texture. Nowadays farmed salmon is available all year round – wild salmon is at its best from February to August.

SARDINE Sea fish. Suitable for grilling or frying. Sardines are young pilchards, sprats or herrings. Available all year round.

SPRAT Sea fish. Suitable for frying or grilling. A small fish similar to herring and at its best from November to March.

BROWN TROUT Freshwater fish. Suitable for grilling or frying. The darker pink/red flesh is considered to be better than that of rainbow trout. At its best from March to September.

RAINBOW TROUT Freshwater fish. Suitable for grilling, frying, poaching and baking. Can be cooked whole or in fillets. Has a delicate pale pink flesh. Available all year round.

SALMON TROUT Freshwater fish. Suitable for poaching or baking whole. Cutlets or fillets can be fried, grilled or griddled. At its best from March to August. Treat as for salmon. Has a pinker flesh than salmon and the flavour is not as good.

TUNA Sea fish (mostly). Suitable for all methods of cooking. Does not count as an oily fish when canned. Available all year round.

Seafood

Crustaceans, such as lobsters, have hard shells which they shed and replace during their lifetime. Molluscs are animals that have hinged shells, such as scallops, or single shells, such as whelks. This term also includes cephalopods such as squid, cuttlefish and octopus.

CLAM Available all year round but best in September. Usually eaten raw like oysters, or cook as for mussels.

COCKLES Available all year round, but best in September.

Normally eaten cooked. Eat plain with vinegar or use in recipes such as paella.

CRAB Best from May to August, but also available canned and frozen. Normally sold ready-cooked either whole or as dressed crab.

CRAWFISH Also known as langoustines. Available all year round, usually imported frozen. Has no claws and is the size of a small lobster.

CRAYFISH Available from September to April. Resemble mini-lobsters and have a delicate flavour.

MUSSELS Best from September to March, but available most of the year due to farming. Normally sold live and can be eaten raw or cooked.

OYSTERS Available from September to April. Usually eaten raw on day of purchase, but can be cooked. Must be eaten absolutely fresh.

DUBLIN BAY PRAWNS Available all year round. Sold live or cooked. Other large prawns are often confused for them.

TIGER PRAWNS Available all year round, raw or cooked. Just one of many varieties of large prawns that are now imported. They are grey when raw and turn pink once cooked. Use within one day of purchasing if live or thawed.

SHRIMP/PRAWNS Available all year round, fresh or frozen.

Shrimp are the smaller of the two and are not used as much in everyday cooking. Shrimp are brown in colour prior to cooking and prawns are grey, both tuning pink once cooked.

SCALLOPS Best from October to March, but available frozen all year. Usually sold live on the shell, but can be bought off the shell, often frozen. Scallops have a bright orange core which is edible. Serve cooked.

SQUID/OCTOPUS Available all year round, sold fresh but previously frozen. Their black ink is often used in sauces, and is also used to make black pasta.

WHELKS Best from September to February. Usually sold cooked and shelled and served with vinegar.

WINKLES Best from October to May. Can be sold cooked or raw. Normally served cooked and with vinegar.

Soups, Salads & Starters

Smoked Salmon Sushi

SERVES 4

175 g/6 oz sushi rice	2 sheets sushi nori	**To serve:**
2 tbsp rice vinegar	60 g/2½ oz smoked salmon	wasabi
4 tsp caster sugar	¼ cucumber, cut into	soy sauce
½ tsp salt	fine strips	pickled ginger

Rinse the rice thoroughly in cold water, until the water runs clear, then place in a pan with 300 ml/½ pint of water. Bring to the boil and cover with a tight-fitting lid. Reduce to a simmer and cook gently for 10 minutes. Turn the heat off, but keep the pan covered, to allow the rice to steam for a further 10 minutes.

In a small saucepan gently heat the rice vinegar, sugar and salt until the sugar has dissolved. When the rice has finished steaming, pour over the vinegar mixture and stir well to mix. Empty the rice out on to a large flat surface (a chopping board or large plate is ideal). Fan the rice to cool and to produce a shinier rice.

Lay one sheet of sushi nori on a sushi mat (if you do not have a sushi mat, improvise with a stiff piece of fabric that is a little larger than the sushi nori) and spread with half the cooled rice. Dampen the hands while doing this (this helps to prevent the rice from sticking to the hands). On the nearest edge place half the salmon and half the cucumber strips.

Roll up the rice and smoked salmon into a tight Swiss roll-like shape. Dampen the blade of a sharp knife and cut the sushi into slices about 2 cm/¾ inch thick. Repeat with the remaining sushi nori, rice, smoked salmon and cucumber. Serve with wasabi, soy sauce and pickled ginger.

Try This: FOR A MORE SUBSTANTIAL OPTION: 104 FOR AN ALTERNATIVE: 28

Salmon Fish Cakes

SERVES 4

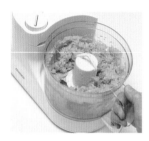

225 g/8 oz potatoes, peeled
450 g/1 lb salmon
   fillet, skinned
125 g/4 oz carrot, trimmed
   and peeled
2 tbsp grated lemon rind

2–3 tbsp freshly
   chopped coriander
1 medium egg yolk
salt and freshly ground
   black pepper
2 tbsp plain white flour

few fine sprays of oil

To serve:
prepared tomato sauce
tossed green salad
crusty bread

Cube the potatoes and cook in lightly salted boiling water for 15 minutes. Drain and mash the potatoes. Place in a mixing bowl and reserve.

Place the salmon in a food processor and blend to form a chunky purée. Add the purée to the potatoes and mix together.

Coarsely grate the carrot and add to the fish with the lemon rind and the coriander.

Add the egg yolk, season to taste with salt and pepper, then gently mix the ingredients together. With damp hands form the mixture into 4 large fish cakes.

Coat in the flour and place on a plate. Cover loosely and chill for at least 30 minutes.

When ready to cook, spray a griddle pan with a few fine sprays of oil and heat the pan. When hot add the fish cakes and cook on both sides for 3–4 minutes or until the fish is cooked. Add an extra spray of oil if needed during the cooking.

When the fish cakes are cooked, serve immediately with the tomato sauce, green salad and crusty bread.

Try This: FOR A MORE SUBSTANTIAL OPTION: 114 FOR AN ALTERNATIVE: 48

Creamy Salmon
with Dill in Filo Baskets

SERVES 4

1 bay leaf
6 black peppercorns
1 large sprig fresh parsley
175 g/6 oz salmon fillet
4 large sheets filo pastry

fine spray of oil
125 g/4 oz baby spinach
   leaves
8 tbsp fromage frais
2 tsp Dijon mustard

2 tbsp freshly chopped dill
salt and freshly ground
   black pepper

Preheat the oven to 200°C/400°F/Gas Mark 6. Place the bay leaf, peppercorns, parsley and salmon in a frying pan and add enough water to barely cover the fish.

Bring to the boil, reduce the heat and poach the fish for 5 minutes until it flakes easily. Remove it from the pan. Reserve.

Spray each sheet of filo pastry lightly with the oil. Scrunch up the pastry to make a nest shape approximately 12.5 cm/5 inches in diameter.

Place on a lightly oiled baking sheet and cook in the preheated oven for 10 minutes until golden and crisp.

Blanch the spinach in a pan of lightly salted boiling water for 2 minutes. Drain thoroughly and keep warm.

Mix the fromage frais, mustard and dill together, then warm gently. Season to taste with salt and pepper. Divide the spinach between the filo pastry nests and flake the salmon on to the spinach.

Spoon the mustard and dill sauce over the filo baskets and serve immediately.

Try This: FOR A MORE SUBSTANTIAL OPTION: 96   FOR AN ALTERNATIVE: 62

Smoked Mackerel Vol–au–Vents

SERVES -1-2

350 g/12 oz prepared
  puff pastry
1 small egg, beaten
2 tsp sesame seeds
225 g/8 oz peppered

smoked mackerel,
  skinned and chopped
5 cm/2 inch piece cucumber
4 tbsp soft cream cheese
2 tbsp cranberry sauce

1 tbsp freshly chopped dill
1 tbsp finely grated
  lemon rind
dill sprigs, to garnish
mixed salad leaves, to serve

Preheat the oven to 230°C/450°F/Gas Mark 8. Roll the pastry out on a lightly floured surface and using a 9 cm/3½ inch fluted cutter cut out 12 rounds.

Using a 1 cm/½ inch cutter mark a lid in the centre of each round. Place on a damp baking sheet and brush the rounds with a little beaten egg. Sprinkle the pastry with the sesame seeds and bake in the preheated oven for 10–12 minutes, or until golden brown and well risen.

Transfer the vol-au-vents to a chopping board and when cool enough to touch carefully remove the lids with a small sharp knife.

Scoop out any uncooked pastry from the inside of each vol-au-vent, then return to the oven for 5–8 minutes to dry out. Remove and allow to cool.

Flake the mackerel into small pieces and reserve. Peel the cucumber if desired, cut into very small dice and add to the mackerel.

Beat the soft cream cheese with the cranberry sauce, dill and lemon rind. Stir in the mackerel and cucumber and use to fill the vol-au-vents. Place the lids on top and garnish with dill sprigs.

Try This: FOR A MORE SUBSTANTIAL OPTION: 34 FOR AN ALTERNATIVE: 32

Smoked Mackerel & Potato Salad

SERVES 4

½ tsp dry mustard powder
1 large egg yolk
salt and freshly ground
   black pepper
150 ml/¼ pint sunflower oil
1–2 tbsp lemon juice

450 g/1 lb baby new
   potatoes
25 g/1 oz butter
350 g/12 oz smoked
   mackerel fillets
4 celery stalks, trimmed and

   finely chopped
3 tbsp creamed horseradish
150 ml/¼ pint crème fraîche
1 Little Gem, rinsed and
   roughly torn
8 cherry tomatoes, halved

Place the mustard powder and egg yolk in a small bowl with salt and pepper and whisk until blended. Add the oil, drop by drop, into the egg mixture, whisking continuously. When the mayonnaise is thick, add the lemon juice, drop by drop, until a smooth, glossy consistency is formed. Reserve.

Cook the potatoes in boiling salted water until tender, then drain. Cool slightly, then cut into halves or quarters, depending on size. Return to the saucepan and toss in the butter.

Remove the skin from the mackerel fillets and flake into pieces. Add to the potatoes in the saucepan, together with the celery.

Blend 4 tablespoons of the mayonnaise with the horseradish and crème fraîche. Season to taste with salt and pepper, then add to the potato and mackerel mixture and stir lightly.

Arrange the lettuce and tomatoes on 4 serving plates. Pile the smoked mackerel mixture on top of the lettuce, grind over a little pepper and serve with the remaining mayonnaise.

 Try This: FOR A MORE SUBSTANTIAL OPTION: 278 FOR AN ALTERNATIVE: 34

Marinated Mackerel with Tomato & Basil Salad

SERVES 3

3 mackerel, filleted
3 beefsteak tomatoes, sliced
50 g/2 oz watercress
2 oranges, peeled and
    segmented
75 g/3 oz mozzarella
    cheese, sliced

2 tbsp basil leaves, shredded
sprig of fresh basil, to garnish

For the marinade:
juice of 2 lemons
4 tbsp olive oil
4 tbsp basil leaves

For the dressing:
1 tbsp lemon juice
1 tsp Dijon mustard
1 tsp caster sugar
salt and freshly ground
    black pepper
5 tbsp olive oil

Remove as many of the fine pin bones as possible from the mackerel fillets, lightly rinse and pat dry with absorbent kitchen paper and place in a shallow dish.

Blend the marinade ingredients together and pour over the mackerel fillets. Make sure the marinade has covered the fish completely. Cover and leave in a cool place for at least 8 hours, but preferably overnight. As the fillets marinate, they will loose the translucency and look as if they are cooked.

Place the tomatoes, watercress, oranges and mozzarella cheese in a large bowl and toss.

To make the dressing, whisk the lemon juice with the mustard, sugar and seasoning in a bowl. Pour over half the dressing, toss again and then arrange on a serving platter. Remove the mackerel from the marinade, cut into bite-sized pieces and sprinkle with the shredded basil. Arrange on top of the salad, drizzle over the remaining dressing, scatter with basil leaves and garnish with a basil sprig. Serve.

Try This: FOR A MORE SUBSTANTIAL OPTION: 124   FOR AN ALTERNATIVE: 52

Sardines in Vine Leaves

SERVES 4

8–16 vine leaves in brine,
   drained
2 spring onions
6 tbsp olive oil
2 tbsp lime juice
2 tbsp freshly chopped
   oregano

1 tsp mustard powder
salt and freshly ground
   black pepper
8 sardines, cleaned
8 bay leaves
8 sprigs of fresh dill

To garnish:
lime wedges
sprigs of fresh dill

To serve:
olive salad
crusty bread

Preheat the grill and line the grill rack with tinfoil just before cooking. Cut 8 pieces of string about 25.5 cm/10 inches long, and leave to soak in cold water for about 10 minutes. Cover the vine leaves in almost boiling water. Leave for 20 minutes, then drain and rinse thoroughly. Pat the vine leaves dry with absorbent kitchen paper.

Trim the spring onions and finely chop, then place into a small bowl. With a balloon whisk beat in the olive oil, lime juice, oregano, mustard powder and season to taste with salt and pepper. Cover with clingfilm and leave in the refrigerator, until required. Stir the mixture before using.

Prepare the sardines, by making 2 slashes on both sides of each fish and brush with a little of the lime juice mixture. Place a bay leaf and a dill sprig inside each sardine cavity and wrap with 1–2 vine leaves, depending on size. Brush with the lime mixture and tie the vine leaves in place with string.

Grill the fish for 4–5 minutes on each side under a medium heat, brushing with a little more of the lime mixture if necessary. Leave the fish to rest, unwrap and discard the vine leaves.

Garnish with lime wedges and sprigs of fresh dill and serve with the remaining lime mixture, olive salad and crusty bread.

Try This: FOR A MORE SUBSTANTIAL OPTION: 218   FOR AN ALTERNATIVE: 92

Tuna Chowder

SERVES 4

2 tsp oil
1 onion, peeled and
    finely chopped
2 sticks of celery, trimmed
    and finely sliced
1 tbsp plain flour

600 ml/1 pint skimmed milk
200 g can tuna in water
320 g can sweetcorn in
    water, drained
2 tsp freshly chopped thyme
salt and freshly ground

black pepper
pinch cayenne pepper
2 tbsp freshly chopped
    parsley

Heat the oil in a large heavy-based saucepan. Add the onion and celery and gently cook for about 5 minutes, stirring from time to time until the onion is softened. Stir in the flour and cook for about 1 minute to thicken.

Draw the pan off the heat and gradually pour in the milk, stirring throughout.

Add the tuna and its liquid, the drained sweetcorn and the thyme. Mix gently, then bring to the boil. Cover and simmer for 5 minutes. Remove the pan from the heat and season to taste with salt and pepper.

Sprinkle the chowder with the cayenne pepper and chopped parsley. Divide into soup bowls and serve immediately.

Try This: FOR A MORE SUBSTANTIAL OPTION: 208   FOR AN ALTERNATIVE: 42

Fresh Tuna Salad

SERVES 4

225 g/8 oz mixed salad
  leaves
225 g/8 oz baby cherry
  tomatoes, halved
  lengthways
125 g/4 oz rocket leaves,
  washed

2 tbsp groundnut oil
550 g/1¼ lb boned tuna
  steaks, each cut into 4
  small pieces
50 g/2 oz piece fresh
  Parmesan cheese

For the dressing:
8 tbsp olive oil
grated zest and juice of
  2 small lemons
1 tbsp wholegrain mustard
salt and freshly ground
  black pepper

Wash the salad leaves and place in a large salad bowl with the cherry tomatoes and rocket and reserve.

Heat the wok, then add the oil and heat until almost smoking. Add the tuna, skin-side down, and cook for 4–6 minutes, turning once during cooking, or until cooked and the flesh flakes easily. Remove from the heat and leave to stand in the juices for 2 minutes before removing.

Meanwhile make the dressing, place the olive oil, lemon zest and juices and mustard in a small bowl or screw-topped jar and whisk or shake well until well blended. Season to taste with salt and pepper.

Transfer the tuna to a clean chopping board and flake, then add it to the salad and toss lightly.

Using a swivel blade vegetable peeler, peel the piece of Parmesan cheese into shavings. Divide the salad between 4 large serving plates, drizzle the dressing over the salad, then scatter with the Parmesan shavings.

Try This: FOR A MORE SUBSTANTIAL OPTION: 192 FOR AN ALTERNATIVE: 90

Mediterranean Chowder

SERVES 6

1 tbsp olive oil
1 tbsp butter
1 large onion, peeled and
    finely sliced
4 celery stalks, trimmed and
    thinly sliced
2 garlic cloves, peeled and
    crushed
1 bird's-eye chilli, deseeded

and finely chopped
1 tbsp plain flour
225 g/8 oz potatoes,
    peeled and diced
600 ml/1 pint fish or
    vegetable stock
700 g/1½ lb whiting or cod
    fillet cut into 2.5 cm/
    1 inch cubes

2 tbsp freshly chopped
    parsley
125 g/4 oz large peeled prawns
198 g can sweetcorn, drained
salt and freshly ground
    black pepper
150 ml/¼ pint single cream
1 tbsp freshly snipped chives
warm, crusty bread, to serve

Heat the oil and butter together in a large saucepan, add the onion, celery and garlic and cook gently for 2–3 minutes until softened. Add the chilli and stir in the flour. Cook, stirring, for a further minute.

Add the potatoes to the saucepan with the stock. Bring to the boil, cover and simmer for 10 minutes. Add the fish cubes to the saucepan with the chopped parsley and cook for a further 5–10 minutes, or until the fish and potatoes are just tender.

Stir in the peeled prawns and sweetcorn and season to taste with salt and pepper. Pour in the cream and adjust the seasoning, if necessary.

Scatter the snipped chives over the top of the chowder. Ladle into 6 large bowls and serve immediately with plenty of warm crusty bread.

Try This: FOR A MORE SUBSTANTIAL OPTION: 306   FOR AN ALTERNATIVE: 86

Poached Fish Dumplings with Creamy Chilli Sauce

SERVES 4

450 g/1 lb white fish fillet, skinned and boned
1 tsp dark soy sauce
1 tbsp cornflour
1 medium egg yolk
salt and freshly ground black pepper
3 tbsp freshly chopped coriander, plus extra, to garnish
1.6 litres/2¾ pints fish stock

For the creamy chilli sauce:
2 tsp groundnut oil
2 garlic cloves, peeled and finely chopped
4 spring onions, trimmed and finely sliced
2 tbsp dry sherry
1 tbsp sweet chilli sauce
1 tbsp light soy sauce
1 tbsp lemon juice
6 tbsp crème fraîche

To garnish:
sprigs of fresh coriander
fresh carrot sticks

Chop the fish into chunks and place in a food processor with the soy sauce, cornflour and egg yolk. Season to taste with salt and pepper. Blend until fairly smooth. Add the coriander and process for a few seconds until well mixed. Transfer to a bowl, cover and chill in the refrigerator for 30 minutes.

With damp hands shape the chilled mixture into walnut-sized balls and place on a baking tray lined with nonstick baking paper. Chill in the refrigerator for a further 30 minutes.

Pour the stock into a wide saucepan, bring to the boil, then reduce the heat until barely simmering. Add the fish balls and poach for 3–4 minutes or until cooked through.

Meanwhile, make the sauce. Heat the oil in a small saucepan, add the garlic and spring onions and cook until golden. Stir in the sherry, chilli and soy sauces and lemon juice, then remove immediately from the heat. Stir in the crème fraîche and season to taste with salt and pepper.

Using a slotted spoon, lift the cooked fish balls from the stock and place on a warmed serving dish. Drizzle over the sauce, garnish with sprigs of fresh coriander and serve immediately.

Try This: FOR A MORE SUBSTANTIAL OPTION: 210   FOR AN ALTERNATIVE: 76

Sweet-&-Sour Battered Fish

SERVES 4-6

450 g/1 lb cod fillet, skinned
150 g/5 oz plain flour
salt and freshly ground
    black pepper
2 tbsp cornflour
2 tbsp arrowroot

vegetable oil for deep-frying

For the sweet-&-sour sauce:
4 tbsp orange juice
2 tbsp white wine vinegar
2 tbsp dry sherry

1 tbsp dark soy sauce
1 tbsp soft light brown sugar
2 tsp tomato purée
1 red pepper, deseeded and
    diced
2 tsp cornflour

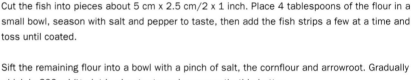

Cut the fish into pieces about 5 cm x 2.5 cm/2 x 1 inch. Place 4 tablespoons of the flour in a small bowl, season with salt and pepper to taste, then add the fish strips a few at a time and toss until coated.

Sift the remaining flour into a bowl with a pinch of salt, the cornflour and arrowroot. Gradually whisk in 300 ml/½ pint iced water to make a smooth, thin batter.

Heat the oil in a wok or deep-fat fryer to 190˚C/ 375˚F. Working in batches, dip the fish strips in the batter and deep-fry them for 3–5 minutes, or until crisp. Using a slotted spoon, remove the strips and drain on absorbent kitchen paper.

Meanwhile, make the sauce. Place 3 tablespoons of the orange juice, the vinegar, sherry, soy sauce, sugar, tomato purée and red pepper in a small saucepan. Bring to the boil, lower the heat and simmer for 3 minutes.

Blend the cornflour with the remaining orange juice, stir into the sauce and simmer, stirring, for 1 minute or until thickened. Arrange the fish on a warmed platter or individual plates. Drizzle a little of the sauce over and serve immediately with the remaining sauce.

Try This: FOR A MORE SUBSTANTIAL OPTION: 258   FOR AN ALTERNATIVE: 62

Thai Fish Cakes

SERVES 4

1 red chilli, deseeded and roughly chopped
4 tbsp roughly chopped fresh coriander
1 garlic clove, peeled and crushed
2 spring onions, trimmed

and roughly chopped
1 lemon grass, outer leaves discarded and roughly chopped
75 g/3 oz prawns, thawed if frozen
275 g/10 oz cod fillet,

skinned, pin bones removed and cubed
salt and freshly ground black pepper
sweet chilli dipping sauce, to serve

Preheat the oven to 190°C/375°F/Gas Mark 5. Place the chilli, coriander, garlic, spring onions and lemon grass in a food processor and blend together.

Pat the prawns and cod dry with kitchen paper.

Add to the food processor and blend until the mixture is roughly chopped.

Season to taste with salt and pepper and blend to mix.

Dampen the hands, then shape heaped tablespoons of the mixture into 12 little patties.

Place the patties on a lightly oiled baking sheet and cook in the preheated oven for 12–15 minutes or until piping hot and cooked through. Turn the patties over halfway through the cooking time.

Serve the fish cakes immediately with the sweet chilli sauce for dipping.

Try This: FOR A MORE SUBSTANTIAL OPTION: 308   FOR AN ALTERNATIVE: 82

Pumpkin & Smoked Haddock Soup

SERVES 4-6

2 tbsp olive oil
1 medium onion,
   peeled and chopped
2 garlic cloves,
   peeled and chopped
3 celery stalks,
   trimmed and chopped

700 g/1½ lb pumpkin,
   peeled, deseeded and
   cut into chunks
450 g/1 lb potatoes, peeled
   and cut into chunks
750 ml/1¼ pints chicken
   stock, heated

125 ml/4 fl oz dry sherry
200 g/7 oz smoked
   haddock fillet
150 ml/¼ pint milk
freshly ground black pepper
2 tbsp freshly chopped
   parsley

Heat the oil in a large heavy-based saucepan and gently cook the onion, garlic and celery for about 10 minutes. This will release the sweetness but not colour the vegetables. Add the pumpkin and potatoes to the saucepan and stir to coat the vegetables with the oil.

Gradually pour in the stock and bring to the boil. Cover, then reduce the heat and simmer for 25 minutes, stirring occasionally. Stir in the dry sherry, then remove the saucepan from the heat and leave to cool for 5–10 minutes.

Blend the mixture in a food processor or blender to form a chunky purée and return to the cleaned saucepan.

Meanwhile, place the fish in a shallow frying pan. Pour in the milk with 3 tablespoons of water and bring to almost boiling point. Reduce the heat, cover and simmer for 6 minutes, or until the fish is cooked and flakes easily. Remove from the heat and, using a slotted spoon, remove the fish from the liquid, reserving both liquid and fish.

Discard the skin and any bones from the fish and flake into pieces. Stir the fish liquid into the soup, together with the flaked fish. Season with freshly ground black pepper, stir in the parsley and serve immediately.

Try This: FOR A MORE SUBSTANTIAL OPTION: 228 FOR AN ALTERNATIVE: 88

Fried Whitebait with Rocket Salad

SERVES 4

450 g/1 lb whitebait, fresh or frozen
oil, for frying
85 g/3 oz plain flour
½ tsp of cayenne pepper
salt and freshly ground

black pepper

For the salad:
125 g/4 oz rocket leaves
125 g/4 oz cherry tomatoes, halved

75 g/3 oz cucumber, cut into dice
3 tbsp olive oil
1 tbsp fresh lemon juice
½ tsp Dijon mustard
½ tsp caster sugar

If the whitebait are frozen, thaw completely, then wipe dry with absorbent kitchen paper.

Start to heat the oil in a deep-fat fryer. Arrange the fish in a large, shallow dish and toss well in the flour, cayenne pepper and salt and pepper.

Deep fry the fish in batches for 2–3 minutes, or until crisp and golden. Keep the cooked fish warm while deep frying the remaining fish.

Meanwhile, to make the salad, arrange the rocket leaves, cherry tomatoes and cucumber on individual serving dishes. Whisk the olive oil and the remaining ingredients together and season lightly. Drizzle the dressing over the salad and serve with the whitebait.

Try This: FOR A MORE SUBSTANTIAL OPTION: 148   FOR AN ALTERNATIVE: 62

Prawn & Chilli Soup

SERVES 4

2 spring onions, trimmed
225 g/8 oz whole raw tiger
   prawns
750 ml/1¼ pint fish stock
finely grated rind and juice

of 1 lime
1 tbsp fish sauce
1 red chilli, deseeded and
   chopped
1 tbsp soy sauce

1 lemon grass stalk
2 tbsp rice vinegar
4 tbsp freshly chopped
   coriander

To make spring onion curls, finely shred the spring onions lengthways. Place in a bowl of iced cold water and reserve.

Remove the heads and shells from the prawns leaving the tails intact.

Split the prawns almost in two to form a butterfly shape and individually remove the black thread that runs down the back of each one.

In a large pan heat the stock with the lime rind and juice, fish sauce, chilli and soy sauce.

Bruise the lemon grass by crushing it along its length with a rolling pin, then add to the stock mixture. When the stock mixture is boiling add the prawns and cook until they are pink.

Remove the lemon grass and add the rice vinegar and coriander. Ladle into bowls and garnish with the spring onion curls. Serve immediately.

Try This: FOR A MORE SUBSTANTIAL OPTION: 290   FOR AN ALTERNATIVE: 56

Thai Hot-&-Sour Prawn Soup

SERVES 6

700 g/1½ lb large raw prawns

2 tbsp vegetable oil

3–4 stalks lemon grass, outer leaves discarded and coarsely chopped

2.5 cm/1 inch piece fresh root ginger, peeled and finely chopped

2–3 garlic cloves, peeled and crushed

small bunch fresh coriander, leaves stripped and reserved, stems finely chopped

½ tsp freshly ground black pepper

1.8 litres/3¼ pints water

1–2 small red chillies, deseeded and thinly sliced

1–2 small green chillies, deseeded and thinly sliced

6 kaffir lime leaves, thinly shredded

4 spring onions, trimmed and diagonally sliced

1–2 tbsp Thai fish sauce

1–2 tbsp freshly squeezed lime juice

Remove the heads from the prawns by twisting away from the body and reserve. Peel the prawns, leaving the tails on and reserve the shells with the heads. Using a sharp knife, remove the black vein from the back of the prawns. Rinse and dry the prawns and reserve. Rinse and dry the heads and shells.

Heat a wok, add the oil and, when hot, add the prawn heads and shells, the lemon grass, ginger, garlic, coriander stems and black pepper and stir-fry for 2–3 minutes, or until the prawn heads and shells turn pink and all the ingredients are coloured.

Carefully add the water to the wok and return to the boil, skimming off any scum which rises to the surface. Simmer over a medium heat for 10 minutes or until slightly reduced. Strain through a fine sieve and return the clear prawn stock to the wok.

Bring the stock back to the boil and add the reserved prawns, chillies, lime leaves and spring onions and simmer for 3 minutes, or until the prawns turn pink. Season with the fish sauce and lime juice. Spoon into heated soup bowls, dividing the prawns evenly and float a few coriander leaves over the surface.

Try This: FOR A MORE SUBSTANTIAL OPTION: 296   FOR AN ALTERNATIVE: 60

Hot Tiger Prawns with Parma Ham

SERVES 4

½ cucumber, peeled if preferred
4 ripe tomatoes
12 raw tiger prawns
6 tbsp olive oil

4 garlic cloves, peeled and crushed
4 tbsp freshly chopped parsley
salt and freshly ground black pepper

6 slices of Parma ham, cut in half
4 slices flat Italian bread
4 tbsp dry white wine

Preheat oven to 180°C/350°F/Gas Mark 4. Slice the cucumber and tomatoes thinly, then arrange on 4 large plates and reserve. Peel the prawns, leaving the tail shell intact and remove the thin black vein running down the back.

Whisk together 4 tablespoons of the olive oil, garlic and chopped parsley in a small bowl and season to taste with plenty of salt and pepper. Add the prawns to the mixture and stir until they are well coated. Remove the prawns, then wrap each one in a piece of Parma ham and secure with a cocktail stick.

Place the prepared prawns on a lightly oiled baking sheet or dish with the slices of bread and cook in the preheated oven for 5 minutes.

Remove the prawns from the oven and spoon the wine over the prawns and bread. Return to the oven and cook for a further 10 minutes until piping hot.

Carefully remove the cocktail sticks and arrange 3 prawn rolls on each slice of bread. Place on top of the sliced cucumber and tomatoes and serve immediately.

Try This: FOR A MORE SUBSTANTIAL OPTION: 292 FOR AN ALTERNATIVE: 72

Quick Mediterranean Prawns

SERVES 4

20 raw Mediterranean
  prawns
3 tbsp olive oil
1 garlic clove, peeled and
  crushed
finely grated zest and juice
  of ½ lemon

sprigs of fresh rosemary

**For the pesto and sun-dried
tomato dips:**
150 ml/¼ pint Greek style
  yoghurt
1 tbsp prepared pesto

150 ml/¼ pint crème fraîche
1 tbsp sun-dried tomato
  paste
1 tbsp wholegrain mustard
salt and freshly ground
  black pepper
lemon wedges, to garnish

Remove the shells from the prawns, leaving the tail shells. Using a small, sharp knife, remove the dark vein that runs along the back of the prawns. Rinse and drain on absorbent kitchen paper.

Whisk 2 tablespoons of the oil with the garlic, lemon zest and juice in a small bowl. Bruise 1 sprig of rosemary with a rolling pin and add to the bowl. Add the prawns, toss to coat, then cover and leave to marinate in the refrigerator until needed.

For the simple dips, mix the yoghurt and pesto in one bowl and the crème fraîche, tomato paste and mustard in another bowl. Season to taste with salt and pepper.

Heat a wok, add the remaining oil and swirl round to coat the sides. Remove the prawns from the marinade, leaving any juices and the rosemary behind. Add to the wok and stir-fry over a high heat for 3–4 minutes, or until the prawns are pink and just cooked through.

Remove the prawns from the wok and arrange on a platter. Garnish with lemon wedges and more fresh rosemary sprigs and serve hot or cold with the dips.

Try This: FOR A MORE SUBSTANTIAL OPTION: 198 FOR AN ALTERNATIVE: 68

Tempura

SERVES 4

For the batter:
200 g/7 oz plain flour
pinch of bicarbonate of soda
1 medium egg yolk

For the prawns & vegetables:
8–12 raw king-size prawns

1 carrot, peeled
125 g/4 oz button
   mushrooms, wiped
1 green pepper, deseeded
1 small aubergine, trimmed
1 onion, peeled
125 g/4 oz French beans

125 ml/4 fl oz sesame oil
300 ml/½ pint vegetable oil
   for deep frying

To serve:
soy sauce
chilli dipping sauce

Sift the flour and bicarbonate of soda into a mixing bowl. Blend 450 ml/¾ pint water and the egg yolk together, then gradually whisk into the flour mixture until a smooth batter is formed.

Peel the prawns, leaving the tails intact, de-vein, then rinse lightly and pat dry with absorbent kitchen paper and reserve. Slice the carrot thinly then, using small pastry cutters, cut out fancy shapes. Cut the mushrooms in half, if large, and cut the pepper into chunks. Slice the aubergine, then cut into chunks, together with the onion, and finally trim the French beans.

Pour the sesame oil and the vegetable oil into a large wok and heat to 180°C/350°F, or until a small spoonful of the batter dropped into the oil sizzles and cooks on impact.

Dip the prawns and vegetables into the reserved batter (no more than 8 pieces at a time) and stir until lightly coated. Cook for 3 minutes, turning occasionally during cooking, or until evenly golden. Using a slotted spoon, transfer the prawns and vegetables onto absorbent kitchen paper and drain well. Keep warm. Repeat with the remaining ingredients. Serve immediately with soy sauce and chilli dipping sauce.

Try This: FOR A MORE SUBSTANTIAL OPTION: 244   FOR AN ALTERNATIVE: 80

Sesame Prawns

SERVES 6-8

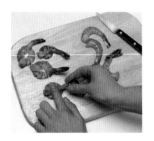

24 large raw prawns
40 g/1 oz plain flour
4 tbsp sesame seeds
salt and freshly ground
black pepper
1 large egg

300 ml/½ pint vegetable oil
for deep frying

For the soy dipping sauce:
50 ml/2 fl oz soy sauce
1 spring onion, trimmed and

finely chopped
½ tsp dried crushed chillies
1 tbsp sesame oil
1–2 tsp sugar, or to taste
strips of spring onion,
to garnish

Remove the heads from the prawns by twisting away from the body and discard. Peel the prawns, leaving the tails on for presentation. Using a sharp knife, remove the black vein from the back of the prawns. Rinse and dry. Slice along the back, but do not cut through the prawn body. Place on the chopping board and press firmly to flatten slightly, to make a butterfly shape.

Put the flour, half the sesame seeds, salt and pepper into a food processor and blend for 30 seconds. Tip into a polythene bag and add the prawns, 4–5 at a time. Twist to seal, then shake to coat with the flour.

Beat the egg in a small bowl with the remaining sesame seeds, salt and pepper.

Heat the oil in a large wok to 190˚C/375˚F, or until a small cube of bread browns in about 30 seconds. Working in batches of 5 or 6, and holding each prawn by the tail, dip into the beaten egg, then carefully lower into the oil. Cook for 1–2 minutes, or until crisp and golden, turning once or twice. Using a slotted spoon, remove the prawns, drain on absorbent kitchen paper and keep warm.

To make the dipping sauce, stir together the soy sauce, spring onion, chillies, oil and sugar until the sugar dissolves. Arrange the prawns on a plate, garnish with strips of spring onion and serve immediately.

Try This: FOR A MORE SUBSTANTIAL OPTION: 348 FOR AN ALTERNATIVE: 54

Crispy Prawns with Chinese Dipping Sauce

SERVES 4

450 g/1 lb medium-sized raw prawns, peeled
¼ tsp salt
6 tbsp groundnut oil
2 garlic cloves, peeled and finely chopped
2.5 cm/1 inch piece fresh

root ginger, peeled and finely chopped
1 green chilli, deseeded and finely chopped
4 stems fresh coriander, leaves and stems roughly chopped

For the dipping sauce:
3 tbsp dark soy sauce
3 tbsp rice wine vinegar
1 tbsp caster sugar
2 tbsp chilli oil
2 spring onions, finely shredded

Using a sharp knife, remove the black vein along the back of the prawns. Sprinkle the prawns with the salt and leave to stand for 15 minutes. Pat dry on absorbent kitchen paper.

Heat a wok or large frying pan, add the groundnut oil and when hot, add the prawns and stir-fry in 2 batches for about 1 minute, or until they turn pink and are almost cooked. Using a slotted spoon, remove the prawns and keep warm in a low oven.

Drain the oil from the wok, leaving 1 tablespoon. Add the garlic, ginger and chilli and cook for about 30 seconds. Add the coriander, return the prawns and stir-fry for 1–2 minutes, or until the prawns are cooked through and the garlic is golden. Turn into a warmed serving dish.

For the dipping sauce, using a fork, beat together the soy sauce, rice vinegar, caster sugar and chilli oil in a small bowl.

Stir in the spring onions. Serve immediately with the hot prawns.

Try This: FOR A MORE SUBSTANTIAL OPTION: 314 FOR AN ALTERNATIVE: 64

Honey & Ginger Prawns

SERVES 4

1 carrot
50 g/2 oz bamboo shoots
4 spring onions
1 tbsp clear honey
1 tbsp tomato ketchup
1 tsp soy sauce
2.5 cm/1 inch piece fresh
   root ginger, peeled and

   finely grated
1 garlic clove, peeled
   and crushed
1 tbsp lime juice
175 g/6 oz peeled prawns,
   thawed if frozen
2 heads little gem
   lettuce leaves

2 tbsp freshly chopped
   coriander
salt and freshly ground
   black pepper

To garnish:
fresh coriander sprigs
lime slices

Cut the carrot into matchstick-size pieces, roughly chop the bamboo shoots and finely slice the spring onions.

Combine the bamboo shoots with the carrot matchsticks and spring onions.

In a wok or large frying pan gently heat the honey, tomato ketchup, soy sauce, ginger, garlic and lime juice with 3 tablespoons of water. Bring to the boil.

Add the carrot mixture and stir-fry for 2–3 minutes until the vegetables are hot. Add the prawns and continue to stir-fry for 2 minutes.

Remove the wok or frying pan from the heat and reserve until cooled slightly.

Divide the little gem lettuce into leaves and rinse lightly.

Stir the chopped coriander into the prawn mixture and season to taste with salt and pepper. Spoon into the lettuce leaves and serve immediately garnished with sprigs of fresh coriander and lime slices.

Try This: FOR A MORE SUBSTANTIAL OPTION: 248 FOR AN ALTERNATIVE: 62

Thai Marinated Prawns

SERVES 4

700 g/1½ lb large raw
  prawns, peeled with
  tails left on
2 large eggs
salt
50 g/2 oz cornflour
vegetable oil for deep-frying
lime wedges, to garnish

For the marinade:
2 lemon grass stalks, outer
  leaves discarded and
  bruised
2 garlic cloves, peeled and
  finely chopped
2 shallots, peeled and
  finely chopped

1 red chilli, deseeded and
  chopped
grated zest and juice of 1
  small lime
400 ml/14 fl oz coconut milk

Mix all the marinade ingredients together in a bowl, pressing on the solid ingredients to release their flavours. Season to taste with salt and reserve.

Using a sharp knife, remove the black vein along the back of the prawns and pat dry with absorbent kitchen paper. Add the prawns to the marinade and stir gently until coated evenly. Leave in the marinade for at least 1 hour, stirring occasionally.

Beat the eggs in a deep bowl with a little salt. Place the cornflour in a shallow bowl. Using a slotted spoon or spatula, transfer the prawns from the marinade to the cornflour. Stir gently until the prawns are coated on all sides and shake off any excess.

Holding each prawn by its tail, dip it into the beaten egg, then into the cornflour again, shaking off any excess.

Pour enough oil into a large wok to come 5 cm/2 inches up the sides and place over a high heat. Working in batches of 5 or 6, deep-fry the prawns for 2 minutes, or until pink and crisp, turning once. Using a slotted spoon, remove and drain on absorbent kitchen paper. Keep warm. Arrange on a warmed serving plate and garnish with lime wedges. Serve immediately.

Try This: FOR A MORE SUBSTANTIAL OPTION: 166   FOR AN ALTERNATIVE: 64

Prawn Salad with Toasted Rice

SERVES 4

For the dressing:
50 ml/2 fl oz rice vinegar
1 red chilli, deseeded and
    thinly sliced
7.5 cm/3 inch piece lemon
    grass stalk, bruised
juice of 1 lime
2 tbsp Thai fish sauce
1 tsp sugar, or to taste

For the salad:
350 g/12 oz large raw
    prawns, peeled with tails
    attached, heads removed
cayenne pepper
1 tbsp long-grain white rice
salt and freshly ground
    black pepper
2 tbsp sunflower oil

1 large head Chinese leaves
    or cos lettuce, shredded
½ small cucumber,
    peeled, deseeded and
    thinly sliced
1 small bunch chives, cut
    into 2.5 cm/1 inch pieces
small bunch of mint leaves

Place all the ingredients for the dressing in a small bowl and leave to stand to let the flavours blend together.

Using a sharp knife, split each prawn lengthways in half, leaving the tail attached to one half. Remove any black vein and pat the prawns dry with absorbent kitchen paper. Sprinkle the prawns with a little salt and cayenne pepper and then reserve.

Heat a wok over a high heat. Add the rice and stir-fry until browned and fragrant. Turn into a mortar and cool. Crush gently with a pestle until coarse crumbs form. Wipe the wok clean.

Reheat the wok, add the oil and when hot, add the prawns and stir-fry for 2 minutes, or until pink. Transfer to a plate and season to taste with salt and pepper.

Place the Chinese leaves or lettuce into a salad bowl with the cucumber, chives and mint leaves and toss lightly together. Remove the lemon grass stalk and some of the chilli from the dressing and pour all but 2 tablespoons over the salad and toss until lightly coated. Add the prawns and drizzle with the remaining dressing, then sprinkle with the toasted rice and serve.

Try This: FOR A MORE SUBSTANTIAL OPTION: 130   FOR AN ALTERNATIVE: 74

Thai Prawn & Rice Noodle Salad

SERVES 4

75 g/3 oz rice vermicelli
175 g/6 oz mangetout, cut in
  half crossways
½ cucumber, peeled,
  deseeded and diced
2–3 spring onions, trimmed
  and thinly sliced
  diagonally
16–20 large cooked tiger
  prawns, peeled with tails

left on
2 tbsp chopped unsalted
  peanuts or cashews

For the dressing:
4 tbsp freshly squeezed
  lime juice
3 tbsp Thai fish sauce
1 tbsp sugar
2.5 cm/1 inch piece fresh

root ginger, peeled and
  finely chopped
1 red chilli, deseeded and
  thinly sliced
3–4 tbsp freshly chopped
  coriander or mint

To garnish:
lime wedges
sprigs of fresh mint

Place the vermicelli in a bowl and pour over hot water to cover. Leave to stand for 5 minutes or until softened. Drain, rinse, then drain again and reserve.

Meanwhile, mix all the dressing ingredients in a large bowl until well blended and the sugar has dissolved. Reserve.

Bring a medium saucepan of water to the boil. Add the mangetout, return to the boil and cook for 30–50 seconds. Drain, refresh under cold running water, drain again and reserve.

Stir the cucumber, spring onions and all but 4 of the prawns into the dressing until coated lightly. Add the mangetout and noodles and toss until all the ingredients are mixed evenly.

Spoon the noodle salad onto warmed individual plates. Sprinkle with peanuts or cashews and garnish each dish with a reserved prawn, a lime wedge and a sprig of mint.

Try This: FOR A MORE SUBSTANTIAL OPTION: 154 FOR AN ALTERNATIVE: 68

Sweetcorn & Crab Soup

SERVES 4

450 g/1 lb fresh corn-on-the-cob
1.3 litres/2¼ pints chicken stock
2–3 spring onions, trimmed and finely chopped
1 cm/½ inch piece fresh root ginger, peeled and finely

chopped
1 tbsp dry sherry or Chinese rice wine
2–3 tsp soy sauce
1 tsp soft light brown sugar
salt and freshly ground black pepper
2 tsp cornflour

225 g/8 oz white crabmeat, fresh or canned
1 medium egg white
1 tsp sesame oil
1–2 tbsp freshly chopped coriander

Wash the corns cobs and dry. Using a sharp knife and holding the corn cobs at an angle to the cutting board, cut down along the cobs to remove the kernels, then scrape the cobs to remove any excess milky residue. Put the kernels and the milky residue into a large wok.

Add the chicken stock to the wok and place over a high heat. Bring to the boil, stirring and pressing some of the kernels against the side of the wok to squeeze out the starch to help thicken the soup. Simmer for 15 minutes, stirring occasionally.

Add the spring onions, ginger, sherry or Chinese rice wine, soy sauce and brown sugar to the wok and season to taste with salt and pepper. Simmer for a further 5 minutes, stirring occasionally.

Blend the cornflour with 1 tablespoon of cold water to form a smooth paste and whisk into the soup. Return to the boil, then simmer over medium heat until thickened.

Add the crabmeat, stirring until blended. Beat the egg white with the sesame oil and stir into the soup in a slow steady stream, stirring constantly. Stir in the chopped coriander and serve immediately.

Try This: FOR A MORE SUBSTANTIAL OPTION: 106   FOR AN ALTERNATIVE: 78

Thai Crab Cakes

SERVES 4

225 g/8 oz white and brown
   crabmeat (about
   equivalent to the flesh
   of 2 medium crabs)
1 tsp ground coriander
¼ tsp chilli powder
¼ tsp ground turmeric
2 tsp lime juice

1 tsp soft light brown sugar
2.5 cm/1 inch piece fresh
   root ginger, peeled and
   grated
3 tbsp freshly chopped
   coriander
2 tsp finely chopped
   lemon grass

2 tbsp plain flour
2 medium eggs, separated
50 g/2 oz fresh white
   breadcrumbs
3 tbsp groundnut oil
lime wedges, to garnish
mixed salad leaves, to serve

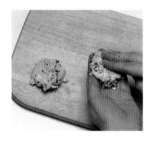

Place the crabmeat in a bowl with the ground coriander, chilli, turmeric, lime juice, sugar, ginger, chopped coriander, lemon grass, flour and egg yolks. Mix together well.

Divide the mixture into 12 equal portions and form each into a small patty about 5 cm/2 inches across. Lightly whisk the egg whites and put into a dish. Place the breadcrumbs on a separate plate.

Dip each crab cake, first in the egg whites, then in the breadcrumbs, turning to coat both sides. Place on a plate, cover and chill in the refrigerator until ready to cook.

Heat the oil in a large frying pan. Add 6 crab cakes and cook for 3 minutes on each side, or until crisp and golden brown on the outside and cooked through. Remove, drain on absorbent kitchen paper and keep warm while cooking the remaining cakes. Arrange on plates, garnish with lime wedges and serve immediately with salad leaves.

Try This: FOR A MORE SUBSTANTIAL OPTION: 126 FOR AN ALTERNATIVE: 56

Deep–fried Crab Wontons

MAKES 24-30

2 tbsp sesame oil
6–8 water chestnuts, rinsed, drained and chopped
2 spring onions, peeled and finely chopped
1 cm/½ inch piece fresh root ginger, peeled and grated
185 g can white crabmeat,

drained
50 ml/2 fl oz soy sauce
2 tbsp rice wine vinegar
½ tsp dried crushed chillies
2 tsp sugar
½ tsp hot pepper sauce, or to taste
1 tbsp freshly chopped

coriander or dill
1 large egg yolk
1 packet wonton skins
vegetable oil for deep-frying
lime wedges, to garnish
dipping sauce, to serve
(see page 66)

Heat a wok or large frying pan, add 1 tablespoon of the sesame oil and when hot, add the water chestnuts, spring onions and ginger and stir-fry for 1 minute. Remove from the heat and leave to cool slightly.

In a bowl, mix the crabmeat with the soy sauce, vinegar, chillies, sugar, hot pepper sauce, coriander or dill and the egg yolk. Stir in the cooled, stir-fried mixture until well blended.

Lay the wonton skins on a work surface and place 1 teaspoonful of the crab mixture on the centre of each. Brush the edges of each wonton skin with a little water and fold up 1 corner to the opposite corner to form a triangle. Press to seal. Bring the 2 corners of the triangle together to meet in the centre, brush 1 with a little water and overlap them, pressing to seal and form a 'tortellini' shape. Place on a baking sheet and continue with the remaining triangles.

Pour enough oil into a large wok to come 5 cm/2 inches up the sides and place over a high heat. Working in batches of 5 or 6, fry the wontons for 3 minutes, or until crisp and golden, turning once or twice. Carefully remove the wontons with a slotted spoon, drain on absorbent kitchen paper and keep warm. Place on individual warmed serving plates, garnish each dish with a lime wedge and serve immediately with the dipping sauce.

Try This: FOR A MORE SUBSTANTIAL OPTION: 182   FOR AN ALTERNATIVE: 48

Seared Scallop Salad

SERVES 4

12 king (large) scallops
1 tbsp margarine or butter
2 tbsp orange juice
2 tbsp balsamic vinegar

1 tbsp clear honey
2 ripe pears, washed
125 g/4 oz rocket
125 g/4 oz watercress

50 g/2 oz walnuts
freshly ground black pepper

Clean the scallops removing the thin black vein from around the white meat and coral. Rinse thoroughly and dry on absorbent kitchen paper. Cut into 2–3 thick slices, depending on the scallop size.

Heat a griddle pan or heavy-based frying pan, then when hot, add the margarine or butter and allow to melt. Once melted, sear the scallops for 1 minute on each side or until golden. Remove from the pan and reserve.

Briskly whisk together the orange juice, balsamic vinegar and honey to make the dressing and reserve.

With a small, sharp knife carefully cut the pears into quarters, core then cut into chunks.

Mix the rocket leaves, watercress, pear chunks and walnuts. Pile on to serving plates and top with the scallops. Drizzle over the dressing and grind over plenty of black pepper. Serve immediately.

Try This: FOR A MORE SUBSTANTIAL OPTION: 256   FOR AN ALTERNATIVE: 42

Warm Lobster Salad
with Hot Thai Dressing

SERVES 4

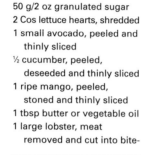

1 orange
50 g/2 oz granulated sugar
2 Cos lettuce hearts, shredded
1 small avocado, peeled and
    thinly sliced
½ cucumber, peeled,
    deseeded and thinly sliced
1 ripe mango, peeled,
    stoned and thinly sliced
1 tbsp butter or vegetable oil
1 large lobster, meat
    removed and cut into bite-

sized pieces
2 tbsp Thai or Italian basil
    leaves
4 large cooked prawns,
    peeled with tails left on,
    to garnish

For the dressing:
1 tbsp vegetable oil
4–6 spring onions, trimmed
    and sliced diagonally into
    5 cm/2 inch pieces

2.5 cm/1 inch piece fresh
    root ginger, peeled and
    grated
1 garlic clove, peeled and
    crushed
grated zest of 1 lime
juice of 2–3 small limes
2 tbsp Thai fish sauce
1 tbsp brown sugar
1–2 tsp sweet chilli sauce,
    or to taste
1 tbsp sesame oil

With a sharp knife, cut the orange rind into thin julienne strips, then cook in boiling water for 2 minutes. Drain the orange strips, then plunge into cold running water, drain and return to the saucepan with the sugar and 1 cm/½ inch water. Simmer until soft, then add 1 tablespoon of cold water to stop cooking. Remove from the heat and reserve. Arrange the lettuce on 4 large plates and arrange the avocado, cucumber and mango slices on top.

Heat a wok or large frying pan, add the butter or oil and when hot, but not sizzling, add the lobster and stir-fry for 1–2 minutes or until heated through. Remove and drain on absorbent kitchen paper.

To make the dressing, heat the vegetable oil in a wok, then add the spring onions, ginger and garlic and stir-fry for 1 minute. Add the lime zest, lime juice, fish sauce, sugar and chilli sauce. Stir until the sugar dissolves. Remove from the heat, add the sesame oil with the orange rind and liquor. Arrange the lobster meat over the salad and drizzle with dressing. Sprinkle with basil leaves, garnish with prawns and serve immediately.

Try This: FOR A MORE SUBSTANTIAL OPTION: 296 FOR AN ALTERNATIVE: 32

Thai Shellfish Soup

SERVES 4-6

350 g/12 oz raw prawns
350 g/12 oz firm white fish, such as monkfish, cod or haddock
175 g/ 6 oz small squid rings
1 tbsp lime juice

450 g/1 lb live mussels
400 ml/15 fl oz coconut milk
1 tbsp groundnut oil
2 tbsp Thai red curry paste
1 lemon grass stalk, bruised
3 kaffir lime leaves, finely

shredded
2 tbsp Thai fish sauce
salt and freshly ground black pepper
fresh coriander leaves, to garnish

Peel the prawns. Using a sharp knife, remove the black vein along the back of the prawns. Pat dry with absorbent kitchen paper and reserve.

Skin the fish, pat dry and cut into 2.5 cm/1 inch chunks. Place in a bowl with the prawns and the squid rings. Sprinkle with the lime juice and reserve.

Scrub the mussels, removing their beards and any barnacles. Discard any mussels that are open, damaged or that do not close when tapped. Place in a large saucepan and add 150 ml/¼ pint of coconut milk. Cover, bring to the boil, then simmer for 5 minutes, or until the mussels open, shaking the saucepan occasionally. Lift out the mussels, discarding any unopened ones, strain the liquid through a muslin-lined sieve and reserve.

Rinse and dry the saucepan. Heat the groundnut oil, add the curry paste and cook for 1 minute, stirring all the time. Add the lemon grass, lime leaves, fish sauce and pour in both the strained and the remaining coconut milk. Bring the contents of the saucepan to a very gentle simmer.

Add the fish mixture to the saucepan and simmer for 2–3 minutes or until just cooked. Stir in the mussels, with or without their shells as preferred. Season to taste with salt and pepper, then garnish with coriander leaves. Ladle into warmed bowls and serve immediately.

Try This: FOR A MORE SUBSTANTIAL OPTION: 280   FOR AN ALTERNATIVE: 42

Hot-&-Sour Squid

SERVES 4

8 baby squid, cleaned
2 tbsp dark soy sauce
2 tbsp hoisin sauce
1 tbsp lime juice
2 tbsp dry sherry
1 tbsp clear honey

2.5 cm/1 inch piece fresh
   root ginger, peeled and
   finely chopped
1 red chilli, deseeded and
   finely chopped
1 green chilli, deseeded and

   finely chopped
1 tsp cornflour
salt and freshly ground
   black pepper
vegetable oil for deep-frying
lime wedges, to garnish

Slice open the body of each squid lengthways, open out and place on a chopping board with the inside uppermost. Using a sharp knife, score lightly in a criss-cross pattern. Cut each one into 4 pieces. Trim the tentacles.

Place the soy and hoisin sauces with the lime juice, sherry, honey, ginger, chillies and cornflour in a bowl. Season to taste with salt and pepper and mix together. Add the squid, stir well to coat, then cover and place in the refrigerator to marinate for 1 hour.

Tip the squid into a sieve over a small saucepan and strain off the marinade. Scrape any bits of chilli or ginger into the saucepan, as they would burn if fried.

Fill a deep-fat fryer one-third full with oil and heat to 180°C/350°F. Deep-fry the squid in batches for 2–3 minutes or until golden and crisp. Remove the squid and drain on absorbent kitchen paper. Keep warm.

Bring the marinade to the boil and let it bubble gently for a few seconds. Arrange the squid on a warmed serving dish and drizzle over the marinade. Garnish with lime wedges and serve immediately.

Try This: FOR A MORE SUBSTANTIAL OPTION: 198   FOR AN ALTERNATIVE: 74

Seafood Noodle Salad

SERVES 4

8 baby squid, cleaned
2 tbsp mirin
2 tbsp rice vinegar
4 tbsp sunflower oil
1 red chilli, deseeded and
   finely chopped
2 garlic cloves, peeled and
   crushed

6 spring onions, trimmed
   and finely sliced
1 red pepper, deseeded and
   finely sliced
1 tbsp turmeric
2 tsp ground coriander
8 raw tiger prawns, peeled
175 g/6 oz medium egg

   noodles
175 g/6 oz fresh white
   crabmeat
50 g/2 oz beansprouts
salt and freshly ground
   black pepper

Remove the tentacles from the squid and reserve. Slit the squid bodies open down one side and open out flat.

Using a small sharp knife, score the flesh diagonally, first in one direction then the other, to make diamond shapes. Place in a bowl with the squid tentacles, mirin, rice vinegar, half the oil and the chilli and leave to marinate in the refrigerator for 1 hour.

Heat a wok until very hot. Add the remaining oil and, when hot, add the garlic, half the spring onions and the red pepper. Stir-fry for 1 minute, then add the turmeric and coriander. Cook for a further 30 seconds before adding the cleaned squid and its marinade and the prawns. Bring to the boil and simmer for 2–3 minutes, or until the squid and prawns are tender. Remove from the heat and leave to cool.

Cook the noodles for 3–4 minutes until tender, or according to packet directions. Drain well and put in a large serving bowl along with the white crabmeat and the cooled squid and prawn mixture. Stir together and leave until cold. Just before serving, add the beansprouts and remaining spring onions with seasoning to taste and serve.

Try This: FOR A MORE SUBSTANTIAL OPTION: 114 FOR AN ALTERNATIVE: 50

Curly Endive & Seafood Salad

SERVES 4

1 head of curly endive
  lettuce
2 green peppers
12.5 cm/5 inch piece
  cucumber
125 g/4 oz squid, cleaned
  and cut into thin rings
225 g/8 oz baby
  asparagus spears

125 g/4 oz smoked salmon
  slices, cut into wide strips
175 g/6 oz fresh cooked
  mussels in their shells

For the lemon dressing:
2 tbsp sunflower oil
1 tbsp white wine vinegar
5 tbsp fresh lemon juice

1–2 tsp caster sugar
1 tsp mild whole-grain
  mustard
salt and freshly ground
  black pepper

To garnish:
slices of lemon
sprigs of fresh coriander

Rinse and tear the endive into small pieces and arrange on a serving platter.

Remove the seeds from the peppers and cut the peppers and the cucumber into small dice. Sprinkle over the endive.

Bring a saucepan of water to the boil and add the squid rings. Bring the pan up to the boil again, then switch off the heat and leave it to stand for 5 minutes. Then drain and rinse thoroughly in cold water.

Cook the asparagus in boiling water for 5 minutes or until tender but just crisp. Arrange with the squid, smoked salmon and mussels on top of the salad.

To make the lemon dressing, put all the ingredients into a screw-topped jar or into a small bowl and mix thoroughly until the ingredients are combined.

Spoon 3 tablespoons of the dressing over the salad and serve the remainder in a small jug. Garnish the salad with slices of lemon and sprigs of coriander and serve.

Try This: FOR A MORE SUBSTANTIAL OPTION: 178   FOR AN ALTERNATIVE: 60

Pasta, Rice & Potatoes

Salmon & Spaghetti in a Creamy Egg Sauce

SERVES 4

3 medium eggs
1 tbsp freshly chopped
  parsley
1 tbsp freshly chopped dill
40 g/1½ oz freshly grated
  Parmesan cheese

40 g/1½ oz freshly grated
  pecorino cheese
2 tbsp dry white wine
freshly ground black pepper
400 g/14 oz spaghetti
350 g/12 oz salmon

fillet, skinned
25 g/1 oz butter
1 tsp olive oil
flat-leaf parsley sprigs,
  to garnish

Beat the eggs in a bowl with the parsley, dill, half of the Parmesan and pecorino cheeses and the white wine. Season to taste with freshly ground black pepper and reserve.

Bring a large pan of lightly salted water to a rolling boil. Add the spaghetti and cook according to the packet instructions, or until 'al dente'.

Meanwhile, cut the salmon into bite-sized pieces. Melt the butter in a large frying pan with the oil and cook the salmon pieces for 3–4 minutes, or until opaque.

Drain the spaghetti thoroughly, return to the pan and immediately add the egg mixture. Remove from the heat and toss well; the eggs will cook in the heat of the spaghetti to make a creamy sauce.

Stir in the remaining cheeses and the cooked pieces of salmon and toss again. Tip into a warmed serving bowl or on to individual plates. Garnish with sprigs of flat-leaf parsley and serve immediately.

Try This: FOR A LIGHTER OPTION: 24 FOR AN ALTERNATIVE: 272

Salmon & Roasted Red Pepper Pasta

SERVES 6

225 g/8 oz skinless and boneless salmon fillet, thinly sliced
3 shallots, peeled and finely chopped
1 tbsp freshly chopped parsley

6 tbsp olive oil
juice of ½ lemon
2 red peppers, deseeded and quartered
handful fresh basil leaves, shredded
50 g/2 oz fresh breadcrumbs

4 tbsp extra virgin olive oil
450 g/1 lb fettuccine or linguine
6 spring onions, trimmed and shredded
salt and freshly ground black pepper

Preheat the grill to high. Place the salmon in a bowl. Add the shallots, parsley, 3 tablespoons of the olive oil and the lemon juice. Reserve.

Brush the pepper quarters with a little olive oil. Cook them under the preheated grill for 8–10 minutes, or until the skins have blackened and the flesh is tender. Place the peppers in a plastic bag until cool enough to handle. When cooled, peel the peppers and cut into strips. Put the strips into a bowl with the basil and the remaining olive oil and reserve.

Toast the breadcrumbs until dry and lightly browned then toss with the extra virgin olive oil and reserve. Bring a large pan of salted water to a rolling boil and add the pasta. Cook according to the packet instructions, or until 'al dente'.

Meanwhile, transfer the peppers and their marinade to a hot frying pan. Add the spring onions and cook for 1–2 minutes, or until they have just softened. Add the salmon and its marinade and cook for a further 1–2 minutes, or until the salmon is just cooked. Season to taste with salt and pepper.

Drain the pasta thoroughly and transfer to a warmed serving bowl. Add the salmon mixture and toss gently. Garnish with the breadcrumbs and serve immediately.

Try This: FOR A LIGHTER OPTION: 26   FOR AN ALTERNATIVE: 102

Salmon &
Mushroom Linguine

SERVES 4

450 g/1 lb salmon fillets, skinned
salt and freshly ground black pepper
75 g/3 oz butter
40 g/1½ oz flour

300 ml/½ pint chicken stock
150 ml/¼ pint whipping cream
225 g/8 oz mushrooms, wiped and sliced
350 g/12 oz linguine

50 g/2 oz Cheddar cheese, grated
50 g/2 oz fresh white breadcrumbs
2 tbsp freshly chopped parsley, to garnish

Preheat the oven to 190°C/375°F/Gas Mark 5, 10 minutes before cooking. Place the salmon in a shallow pan and cover with water. Season well with salt and pepper and bring to the boil, then lower the heat and simmer for 6–8 minutes, or until cooked. Drain and keep warm.

Melt 50 g/2 oz of the butter in a heavy-based pan, stir in the flour, cook for 1 minute then whisk in the chicken stock. Simmer gently until thickened. Stir in the cream and season to taste. Keep the sauce warm.

Melt the remaining butter, in a pan, add the sliced mushrooms and cook for 2–3 minutes. Stir the mushrooms into the white sauce.

Bring a large pan of lightly salted water to a rolling boil. Add the linguine and cook according to the packet instructions, or until 'al dente'.

Drain the pasta thoroughly and return to the pan. Stir in half the sauce, then spoon into a lightly oiled 1.4 litre/2½ pint shallow ovenproof dish. Flake the salmon, add to the remaining sauce then pour over the pasta. Sprinkle with the cheese and breadcrumbs, then bake in the preheated oven for 15–20 minutes, or until golden. Garnish with the parsley and serve immediately.

Try This: FOR A LIGHTER OPTION: 28   FOR AN ALTERNATIVE: 110

Seared Salmon & Lemon Linguine

SERVES 4

4 small skinless salmon
   fillets, each about 75 g/3 oz
2 tsp sunflower oil
½ tsp mixed or black
   peppercorns, crushed
400 g/14 oz linguine
15 g/½ oz unsalted butter

1 bunch spring onions,
   trimmed and shredded
300 ml/½ pint soured cream
zest of 1 lemon, finely
   grated
50 g/2 oz freshly grated
   Parmesan cheese

1 tbsp lemon juice
pinch of salt

To garnish:
dill sprigs
lemon slices

Brush the salmon fillets with the sunflower oil, sprinkle with crushed peppercorns and press on firmly and reserve.

Bring a large pan of lightly salted water to a rolling boil. Add the linguine and cook according to the packet instructions, or until 'al dente'.

Meanwhile, melt the butter in a saucepan and cook the shredded spring onions gently for 2–3 minutes, or until soft. Stir in the soured cream and the lemon zest and remove from the heat.

Preheat a griddle or heavy-based frying pan until very hot. Add the salmon and sear for 1½–2 minutes on each side. Remove from the pan and allow to cool slightly.

Bring the soured cream sauce to the boil and stir in the Parmesan cheese and lemon juice. Drain the pasta thoroughly and return to the pan. Pour over the sauce and toss gently to coat.

Spoon the pasta on to warmed serving plates and top with the salmon fillets. Serve immediately with sprigs of dill and lemon slices.

Try This: FOR A LIGHTER OPTION: 86   FOR AN ALTERNATIVE: 112

Rice with Smoked Salmon & Ginger

SERVES 4

225 g/8 oz basmati rice
600 ml/1 pint fish stock
1 bunch spring onions, trimmed and diagonally sliced
3 tbsp freshly chopped

coriander
1 tsp grated fresh root ginger
200 g/7 oz sliced smoked salmon
2 tbsp soy sauce
1 tsp sesame oil

2 tsp lemon juice
4–6 slices pickled ginger
2 tsp sesame seeds
rocket leaves, to serve

Place the rice in a sieve and rinse under cold water until the water runs clear. Drain, then place in a large saucepan with the stock and bring gently to the boil. Reduce to a simmer and cover with a tight-fitting lid. Cook for 10 minutes, then remove from the heat and leave, covered, for a further 10 minutes.

Stir the spring onions, coriander and fresh ginger into the cooked rice and mix well.

Spoon the rice into 4 tartlet tins, each measuring 10 cm/4 inches, and press down firmly with the back of a spoon to form cakes. Invert a tin onto an individual serving plate, then tap the base firmly and remove the tin. Repeat with the rest of the filled tins.

Top the rice with the salmon, folding if necessary, so the sides of the rice can still be seen in places. Mix together the soy sauce, sesame oil and lemon juice to make a dressing, then drizzle over the salmon. Top with the pickled ginger and a sprinkling of sesame seeds. Scatter the rocket leaves around the edge of the plates and serve immediately.

Try This: FOR A LIGHTER OPTION: 62   FOR AN ALTERNATIVE: 204

Pan–fried Salmon with Herb Risotto

SERVES 4

4 x 175 g/6 oz salmon fillets
3–4 tbsp plain flour
1 tsp dried mustard powder
salt and freshly ground
    black pepper
2 tbsp olive oil
3 shallots, peeled and
    chopped

225 g/8 oz Arborio rice
150 ml/¼ pint dry white wine
1.4 litres/2½ pints vegetable
    or fish stock
50 g/2 oz butter
2 tbsp freshly snipped chives
2 tbsp freshly chopped dill
2 tbsp freshly chopped flat-

leaf parsley
knob of butter

To garnish:
slices of lemon
sprigs of fresh dill
tomato salad, to serve

Wipe the salmon fillets with a clean, damp cloth. Mix together the flour, mustard powder and seasoning on a large plate and use to coat the salmon fillets and reserve.

Heat half the olive oil in a large frying pan and fry the shallots for 5 minutes until softened, but not coloured. Add the rice and stir for 1 minute, then slowly add the wine, bring to the boil and boil rapidly until reduced by half.

Bring the stock to a gentle simmer, then add to the rice, a ladleful at a time. Cook, stirring frequently, until all the stock has been added and the rice is cooked but still retains a bite. Stir in the butter and freshly chopped herbs and season to taste with salt and pepper.

Heat the remaining olive oil and the knob of butter in a large griddle pan, add the salmon fillets and cook for 2–3 minutes on each side, or until cooked. Arrange the herb risotto on warm serving plates and top with the salmon. Garnish with slices of lemon and sprigs of dill and serve immediately with a tomato salad.

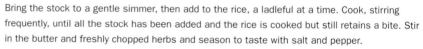

Try This: FOR A LIGHTER OPTION: 28 FOR AN ALTERNATIVE: 306

Salmon & Filo Parcels

SERVES 4

1 tbsp sunflower oil
1 bunch of spring onions, trimmed and finely chopped
1 tsp paprika
175 g/6 oz long-grain

white rice
300 ml/½ pint fish stock
salt and freshly ground black pepper
450 g/1 lb salmon fillet, cubed
1 tbsp freshly chopped parsley

grated rind and juice of 1 lemon
150 g/5 oz rocket
150 g/5 oz spinach
12 sheets filo pastry
50 g/2 oz butter, melted

Preheat the oven to 200°C/400°F/Gas Mark 6. Heat the oil in a small frying pan and gently cook the spring onions for 2 minutes. Stir in the paprika and continue to cook for 1 minute, then remove from the heat and reserve.

Put the rice in a sieve and rinse under cold running water until the water runs clear; drain. Put the rice and stock in a saucepan, bring to the boil, then cover and simmer for 10 minutes, or until the liquid is absorbed and the rice is tender. Add the spring onion mixture and fork through. Season to taste with salt and pepper, then leave to cool.

In a non-metallic bowl, mix together the salmon, parsley, lemon rind and juice and salt and pepper. Reserve. Blanch the rocket and spinach for 30 seconds in a large saucepan of boiling water, or until just wilted. Drain well in a colander and refresh in plenty of cold water, then squeeze out as much moisture as possible.

Brush 3 sheets of filo pastry with melted butter and lay them on top of one another. Take a quarter of the rice mixture and arrange it in an oblong in the centre of the pastry. On top of this place a quarter of the salmon followed by a quarter of the rocket and spinach. Draw up the pastry around the filling and twist at the top to create a parcel. Repeat with the remaining pastry and filling until you have 4 parcels. Brush with the remaining butter. Place on a lightly oiled baking tray and cook in the preheated oven for 20 minutes, or until golden brown. Serve immediately.

Try This: FOR A LIGHTER OPTION: 72   FOR AN ALTERNATIVE: 96

Smoked Salmon with Broad Beans & Rice

SERVES 4

2 tbsp sunflower oil
25 g/1 oz unsalted butter
1 onion, peeled and chopped
2 garlic cloves, peeled
   and chopped
175 g/6 oz asparagus
   tips, halved
75 g/3 oz frozen broad beans

150 ml/¼ pint dry white wine
125 g/4 oz sun-dried
   tomatoes, drained
   and sliced
125 g/4 oz baby spinach
   leaves, washed
450 g/1 lb cooked
   long-grain rice

3 tbsp crème fraîche
225 g/8 oz smoked salmon,
   cut into strips
75 g/3 oz freshly grated
   Parmesan cheese
salt and freshly ground
   black pepper

Heat a large wok, then add the oil and butter and, when melted, stir-fry the onion for 3 minutes, until almost softened. Add the garlic and asparagus tips and stir-fry for 3 minutes. Add the broad beans and wine and bring to the boil, then simmer, stirring occasionally, until the wine is reduced slightly.

Add the sun-dried tomatoes and bring back to the boil, then simmer for 2 minutes. Stir in the baby spinach leaves and cooked rice and return to the boil. Stir-fry for 2 minutes, or until the spinach is wilted and the rice is heated through thoroughly.

Stir in the crème fraîche, smoked salmon strips and Parmesan cheese. Stir well and cook, stirring frequently, until piping hot. Season to taste with salt and pepper. Serve immediately.

Try This: FOR A LIGHTER OPTION: 48   FOR AN ALTERNATIVE: 174

Potato Pancakes with Smoked Salmon

SERVES 4

450 g/1 lb floury potatoes,
    peeled and quartered
salt and freshly ground
    black pepper
1 large egg
1 large egg yolk
25 g/1 oz butter

25 g/1 oz plain flour
150 ml/¼ pint double cream
2 tbsp freshly
    chopped parsley
5 tbsp crème fraîche
1 tbsp horseradish sauce
225 g/8 oz smoked

salmon, sliced
salad leaves, to serve

To garnish:
lemon slices
snipped chives

Cook the potatoes in a saucepan of lightly salted boiling water for 15–20 minutes, or until tender. Drain thoroughly, then mash until free of lumps. Beat in the whole egg and egg yolk, together with the butter. Beat until smooth and creamy. Slowly beat in the flour and cream, then season to taste with salt and pepper. Stir in the chopped parsley.

Beat the crème fraîche and horseradish sauce together in a small bowl, cover with cling-film and reserve.

Heat a lightly oiled, heavy-based frying pan over a medium-high heat. Place a few spoonfuls of the potato mixture in the hot pan and cook for 4–5 minutes, or until cooked and golden, turning halfway through cooking time. Remove from the pan, drain on absorbent kitchen paper and keep warm. Repeat with the remaining mixture.

Arrange the pancakes on individual serving plates. Place the smoked salmon on the pancakes and spoon over a little of the horseradish sauce. Serve with salad and the remaining horseradish sauce and garnish with lemon slices and chives.

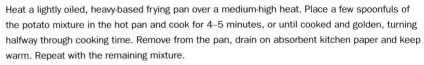

Try This: FOR A LIGHTER OPTION: 92   FOR AN ALTERNATIVE: 114

Salmon with Herbed Potatoes

SERVES 4

450 g/1 lb baby new potatoes

salt and freshly ground black pepper

4 salmon steaks, each weighing about 175 g/6 oz

1 carrot, peeled and cut into fine strips

175 g/6 oz asparagus spears, trimmed

175 g/6 oz sugar snap peas, trimmed

finely grated rind and juice of 1 lemon

25 g/1 oz butter

4 large sprigs of fresh parsley

Preheat the oven to 190°C/375°F/Gas Mark 5, about 10 minutes before required. Parboil the potatoes in lightly salted boiling water for 5–8 minutes until they are barely tender. Drain and reserve.

Cut out 4 pieces of baking parchment paper, measuring 20.5 cm/8 inches square, and place on the work surface. Arrange the parboiled potatoes on top. Wipe the salmon steaks and place on top of the potatoes.

Place the carrot strips in a bowl with the asparagus spears, sugar snaps and grated lemon rind and juice. Season to taste with salt and pepper. Toss lightly together.

Divide the vegetables evenly between the salmon. Dot the top of each parcel with butter and a sprig of parsley.

To wrap a parcel, lift up 2 opposite sides of the paper and fold the edges together. Twist the paper at the other 2 ends to seal the parcel well. Repeat with the remaining parcels.

Place the parcels on a baking tray and bake in the preheated oven for 15 minutes. Place an unopened parcel on each plate and open just before eating.

Try This: FOR A LIGHTER OPTION: 32 FOR AN ALTERNATIVE: 106

Tuna Cannelloni

SERVES 4

1 tbsp olive oil
6 spring onions, trimmed
  and finely sliced
1 sweet Mediterranean red
  pepper, deseeded and
  finely chopped
200 g can tuna in brine

250 g tub ricotta cheese
zest and juice of 1 lemon
1 tbsp freshly snipped chives
salt and freshly ground
  black pepper
8 dried cannelloni tubes
1 medium egg, beaten

125 g/4 oz cottage cheese
150 ml/¼ pint natural yoghurt
pinch of freshly grated
  nutmeg
50 g/2 oz mozzarella
  cheese, grated
tossed green salad, to serve

Preheat oven to 180°C/375°F/Gas Mark 5, 10 minutes before cooking. Heat the olive oil in a frying pan and cook the spring onions and pepper until soft. Remove from the pan with a slotted draining spoon and place in a large bowl.

Drain the tuna, then stir into the spring onions and pepper. Beat the ricotta cheese with the lemon zest and juice and the snipped chives and season to taste with salt and pepper until soft and blended. Add to the tuna and mix together. If the mixture is still a little stiff, add a little extra lemon juice.

With a teaspoon, carefully spoon the mixture into the cannelloni tubes, then lay the filled tubes in a lightly oiled shallow ovenproof dish. Beat the egg, cottage cheese, natural yoghurt and nutmeg together and pour over the cannelloni. Sprinkle with the grated mozzarella cheese and bake in the preheated oven for 15–20 minutes, or until the topping is golden brown and bubbling. Serve immediately with a tossed green salad.

Try This: FOR A LIGHTER OPTION: 40   FOR AN ALTERNATIVE: 206

Tuna & Macaroni Timbales

SERVES 4

125 g/4 oz macaroni
200 g can tuna in brine,
    drained
150 ml/¼ pint single cream
150 ml/¼ pint double cream
50 g/2 oz Gruyère cheese,
    grated

3 medium eggs, lightly beaten
salt and freshly ground
    black pepper
fresh chives, to garnish

For the fresh tomato dressing:
1 tsp Dijon mustard

1 tsp red wine vinegar
2 tbsp sunflower oil
1 tbsp hazelnut or walnut oil
350 g/12 oz firm ripe
    tomatoes, skinned,
    deseeded and chopped
2 tbsp freshly snipped chives

Preheat the oven to 180°C/350°F/Gas Mark 4, 10 minutes before cooking. Oil and line the bases of 4 individual 150 ml/¼ pint timbales or ovenproof cups with non-stick baking parchment and stand in a small roasting tin. Bring a large pan of lightly salted water to a rolling boil. Add the macaroni and cook according to the packet instructions, or until 'al dente'. Drain the cooked pasta thoroughly. Flake the tuna fish and mix with the macaroni. Divide between the timbales or cups.

Pour the single and double cream into a small saucepan. Bring to the boil slowly, remove from the heat and stir in the Gruyère cheese until melted. Allow to cool for 1–2 minutes, then whisk into the beaten egg and season lightly with salt and pepper. Pour the mixture over the tuna fish and macaroni and cover each timbale with a small piece of tinfoil. Pour enough hot water into the roasting tin to come halfway up the timbales. Place in the preheated oven and cook for 25 minutes. Remove the timbales from the water and allow to stand for 5 minutes.

For the tomato dressing, whisk together the mustard and vinegar in a small bowl, using a fork. Gradually whisk in the sunflower and nut oils, then stir in the chopped tomatoes and the snipped chives. Unmould the timbales on to warmed serving plates and spoon the tomato dressing over the top and around the bottom. Garnish with fresh chives and serve immediately.

Try This: FOR A LIGHTER OPTION: 40   FOR AN ALTERNATIVE: 208

Tagliatelle with Tuna & Anchovy Tapenade

SERVES 4

400 g/14 oz tagliatelle
125 g can tuna fish in oil,
    drained
45 g/1¾ oz can anchovy
    fillets, drained

150 g/5 oz pitted black olives
2 tbsp capers in brine,
    drained
2 tsp lemon juice
100 ml/3½ fl oz olive oil

2 tbsp freshly chopped
    parsley
freshly ground black pepper
sprigs of flat-leaf parsley,
    to garnish

Bring a large pan of lightly salted water to a rolling boil. Add the tagliatelle and cook according to the packet instructions, or until 'al dente'.

Meanwhile, place the tuna fish, anchovy fillets, olives and capers in a food processor with the lemon juice and 2 tablespoons of the olive oil and blend for a few seconds until roughly chopped.

With the motor running, pour in the remaining olive oil in a steady stream; the resulting mixture should be slightly chunky rather than smooth.

Spoon the sauce into a bowl, stir in the chopped parsley and season to taste with black pepper. Check the taste of the sauce and add a little more lemon juice, if required.

Drain the pasta thoroughly. Pour the sauce into the pan and cook over a low heat for 1–2 minutes to warm through.

Return the drained pasta to the pan and mix together with the sauce. Tip into a warmed serving bowl or spoon on to warm individual plates. Garnish with sprigs of flat-leaf parsley and serve immediately.

Try This: FOR A LIGHTER OPTION: 82   FOR AN ALTERNATIVE: 276

Tuna Fish Burgers

MAKES 8

450 g/1 lb potatoes, peeled
   and cut into chunks
50 g/2 oz butter
2 tbsp milk
400 g can tuna in oil
1 spring onion, trimmed and
   finely chopped
1 tbsp freshly chopped

parsley
salt and freshly ground
   black pepper
2 medium eggs, beaten
2 tbsp seasoned plain flour
125 g/4 oz fresh white
   breadcrumbs
4 tbsp vegetable oil

4 sesame seed baps
   (optional)

To serve:
fat chips
mixed salad
tomato chutney

Place the potatoes in a large saucepan, cover with boiling water and simmer until soft. Drain, then mash with 40 g/1½ oz of the butter and the milk. Turn into a large bowl. Drain the tuna, discarding the oil and flake into the bowl of potato. Stir well to mix.

Add the spring onions and parsley to the mixture and season to taste with salt and pepper. Add 1 tablespoon of the beaten egg to bind the mixture together. Chill in the refrigerator for at least 1 hour.

Shape the chilled mixture with your hands into 4 large burgers. First, coat the burgers with seasoned flour, then brush them with the remaining beaten egg, allowing any excess to drip back into the bowl. Finally, coat them evenly in the breadcrumbs, pressing the crumbs on with your hands, if necessary.

Heat a little of the oil in a frying pan and fry the burgers for 2–3 minutes on each side until golden, adding more oil if necessary. Drain on absorbent kitchen paper and serve hot in baps, if using, with chips, mixed salad and chutney.

Try This: FOR A LIGHTER OPTION: 40   FOR AN ALTERNATIVE: 210

Smoked Mackerel & Pasta Frittata

SERVES 4

25 g/1 oz tricolore pasta
spirals or shells
225 g/8 oz smoked mackerel
6 medium eggs
3 tbsp milk
2 tsp wholegrain mustard
2 tbsp freshly chopped

parsley
salt and freshly ground
black pepper
25 g/1 oz unsalted butter
6 spring onions, trimmed and
diagonally sliced
50 g/2 oz frozen peas, thawed

75 g/3 oz mature Cheddar
cheese, grated

To serve:
green salad
warm crusty bread

Preheat the grill to high just before cooking. Bring a pan of lightly salted water to a rolling boil. Add the pasta and cook according to the packet instructions, or until 'al dente'. Drain thoroughly and reserve.

Remove the skin from the mackerel and break the fish into large flakes, discarding any bones, and reserve.

Place the eggs, milk, mustard and parsley in a bowl and whisk together. Season with just a little salt and plenty of freshly ground black pepper and reserve.

Melt the butter in a large, heavy-based frying pan. Cook the spring onions gently for 3–4 minutes, until soft. Pour in the egg mixture, then add the drained pasta, peas and half of the mackerel.

Gently stir the mixture in the pan for 1–2 minutes, or until beginning to set. Stop stirring and cook for about 1 minute until the underneath is golden-brown.

Scatter the remaining mackerel over the frittata, followed by the grated cheese. Place under the preheated grill for about 1½ minutes, or until golden-brown and set. Cut into wedges and serve immediately with salad and crusty bread.

Try This: FOR A LIGHTER OPTION: 30 FOR AN ALTERNATIVE: 278

Fettuccine with Sardines & Spinach

SERVES 4

120 g can sardines in olive oil
400 g/14 oz fettuccine or tagliarini
40 g/1½ oz butter
2 tbsp olive oil
50 g/2 oz one-day-old white breadcrumbs
1 garlic clove, peeled and finely chopped
50 g/2 oz pine nuts
125 g/4 oz chestnut mushrooms, wiped and sliced
125 g/4 oz baby spinach leaves, rinsed
150 ml/¼ pint crème fraîche
rind of 1 lemon, finely grated
salt and freshly ground black pepper

Drain the sardines and cut in half lengthwise. Remove the bones, then cut the fish into 2.5 cm/1 inch pieces and reserve.

Bring a large pan of lightly salted water to a rolling boil. Add the pasta and cook according to the packet instructions, or until 'al dente'.

Meanwhile, melt half the butter with the olive oil in a large saucepan, add the breadcrumbs and fry, stirring, until they begin to turn crisp. Add the garlic and pine nuts and continue to cook until golden-brown. Remove from the pan and reserve. Wipe the pan clean.

Melt the remaining butter in the pan, add the mushrooms and cook for 4–5 minutes, or until soft. Add the spinach and cook, stirring, for 1 minute, or until beginning to wilt. Stir in the crème fraîche and lemon rind and bring to the boil. Simmer gently until the spinach is just cooked. Season the sauce to taste with salt and pepper.

Drain the pasta thoroughly and return to the pan. Add the spinach sauce and sardine pieces and gently toss together. Tip into a warmed serving dish. Sprinkle with the toasted breadcrumbs and pine nuts and serve immediately.

Try This: FOR A LIGHTER OPTION: 52   FOR AN ALTERNATIVE: 218

Saucy Cod & Pasta Bake

SERVES 4

450 g/1 lb cod fillets, skinned
2 tbsp sunflower oil
1 onion, peeled and
    chopped
4 rashers smoked streaky
    bacon, rind removed and
    chopped
150 g/5 oz baby button
    mushrooms, wiped

2 celery sticks, trimmed and
    thinly sliced
2 small courgettes, halved
    lengthwise and sliced
400 g can chopped tomatoes
100 ml/3½ fl oz fish stock or
    dry white wine
1 tbsp freshly
    chopped tarragon

salt and freshly ground
    black pepper

For the pasta topping:
225–275 g/8–10 oz pasta
    shells
25 g/1 oz butter
4 tbsp plain flour
450 ml/¾ pint milk

Preheat the oven to 200°C/400°F/Gas Mark 6, 15 minutes before cooking. Cut the cod into bite-sized pieces and reserve.

Heat the sunflower oil in a large saucepan, add the onion and bacon and cook for 7–8 minutes. Add the mushrooms and celery and cook for 5 minutes, or until fairly soft. Add the courgettes and tomatoes to the bacon mixture and pour in the fish stock or wine. Bring to the boil, then simmer uncovered for 5 minutes, or until the sauce has thickened slightly.

Remove from the heat and stir in the cod pieces and the tarragon. Season to taste with salt and pepper, then spoon into a large oiled baking dish. Meanwhile, bring a large pan of lightly salted water to a rolling boil. Add the pasta shells and cook, according to the packet instructions, or until 'al dente'.

For the topping, place the butter and flour in a saucepan and pour in the milk. Bring to the boil slowly, whisking until thickened and smooth. Drain the pasta thoroughly, and stir into the sauce. Spoon carefully over the fish and vegetables. Place in the preheated oven and bake for 20–25 minutes, or until the top is lightly browned and bubbling.

Try This: FOR A LIGHTER OPTION: 44   FOR AN ALTERNATIVE: 222

Crispy Cod Cannelloni

SERVES 4

1 tbsp olive oil
8 dried cannelloni tubes
25 g/1 oz unsalted butter
225 g/8 oz button
    mushrooms, thinly sliced
175 g/6 oz leeks, trimmed
    and finely chopped

175 g/6 oz cod, skinned
    and diced
175 g/6 oz cream cheese
salt and freshly ground black
    pepper
15 g/½ oz Parmesan cheese,
    grated

50 g/2 oz fine fresh white
    breadcrumbs
3 tbsp plain flour
1 medium egg, lightly beaten
oil for deep frying
fresh herbs or salad leaves,
    to serve

Add 1 teaspoon of the olive oil to a large pan of lightly salted water and bring to a rolling boil. Add the cannelloni tubes and cook, uncovered, for 5 minutes. Drain and leave in a bowl of cold water.

Melt the butter with the remaining oil in a saucepan. Add the mushrooms and leeks and cook gently for 5 minutes. Turn up the heat and cook for 1–2 minutes, or until the mixture is fairly dry. Add the cod and cook, stirring, for 2–3 minutes, or until the fish is opaque. Add the cream cheese to the pan and stir until melted. Season to taste with salt and pepper, then leave the cod mixture to cool.

Drain the cannelloni. Using a piping bag without a nozzle or a spoon, fill the cannelloni with the cod mixture.

Mix the Parmesan cheese and breadcrumbs together on a plate. Dip the filled cannelloni into the flour, then into the beaten egg and finally into the breadcrumb mixture. Dip the ends twice to ensure they are thoroughly coated. Chill in the refrigerator for 30 minutes.

Heat the oil for deep frying to 180°C/350°F. Fry the stuffed cannelloni in batches for 2–3 minutes, or until the coating is crisp and golden-brown. Drain on absorbent kitchen paper and serve immediately with fresh herbs or salad leaves.

Try This: FOR A LIGHTER OPTION: 36 FOR AN ALTERNATIVE: 226

Spanish Omelette with Smoked Cod

SERVES 4

3 tbsp sunflower oil
350 g/12 oz potatoes, peeled
and cut into 1 cm/½
inch cubes
2 medium onions, peeled
and cut into wedges
2–4 large garlic cloves,
peeled and thinly sliced
1 large red pepper,

deseeded, quartered and
thinly sliced
125 g/4 oz smoked cod
salt and freshly ground
black pepper
25 g/1 oz butter, melted
1 tbsp double cream
6 medium eggs, beaten
2 tbsp freshly chopped

flat-leaf parsley
50 g/2 oz mature Cheddar
cheese, grated

To serve:
crusty bread
tossed green salad, to serve

Heat the oil in a large non-stick heavy-based frying pan, add the potatoes, onions and garlic and cook gently for 10–15 minutes until golden brown, then add the red pepper and cook for 3 minutes.

Meanwhile, place the fish in a shallow frying pan and cover with water. Season to taste with salt and pepper and poach gently for 10 minutes. Drain and flake the fish into a bowl, toss in the melted butter and cream, adjust the seasoning and reserve.

When the vegetables are cooked, drain off any excess oil and stir in the beaten egg with the chopped parsley. Pour the fish mixture over the top and cook gently for 5 minutes, or until the eggs become firm.

Sprinkle the grated cheese over the top and place the pan under a preheated hot grill. Cook for 2–3 minutes until the cheese is golden and bubbling. Carefully slide the omelette onto a large plate and serve immediately with plenty of bread and salad.

Try This: FOR A LIGHTER OPTION: 78   FOR AN ALTERNATIVE: 224

Spicy Cod Rice

SERVES 4

1 tbsp plain flour
1 tbsp freshly chopped
   coriander
1 tsp ground cumin
1 tsp ground coriander
550 g/1¼ lb thick-cut cod
   fillet, skinned and cut into
   large chunks

4 tbsp groundnut oil
50 g/2 oz cashew nuts
1 bunch spring onions,
   trimmed and
   diagonally sliced
1 red chilli, deseeded
   and chopped
1 carrot, peeled and cut

into matchsticks
125 g/4 oz frozen peas
450 g/1 lb cooked long-
   grain rice
2 tbsp sweet chilli sauce
2 tbsp soy sauce

Mix together the flour, coriander, cumin and ground coriander on a large plate. Coat the cod in the spice mixture then place on a baking sheet, cover and chill in the refrigerator for 30 minutes.

Heat a large wok, then add 2 tablespoons of the oil and heat until almost smoking. Stir-fry the cashew nuts for 1 minute, until browned, then remove and reserve.

Add a further 1 tablespoon of the oil and heat until almost smoking. Add the cod and stir-fry for 2 minutes. Using a fish slice, turn the cod pieces over and cook for a further 2 minutes, until golden. Remove from the wok, place on a warm plate, cover and keep warm.

Add the remaining oil to the wok, heat until almost smoking then stir-fry the spring onions and chilli for 1 minute before adding the carrots and peas and stir-frying for a further 2 minutes. Stir in the rice, chilli sauce, soy sauce and cashew nuts and stir-fry for 3 more minutes. Add the cod, heat for 1 minute, then serve immediately.

Try This: FOR A LIGHTER OPTION: 50   FOR AN ALTERNATIVE: 220

Farfalle with Smoked Trout in a Dill & Vodka Sauce

SERVES 4

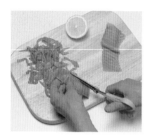

400 g/14 oz farfalle
150 g/5 oz smoked trout
2 tsp lemon juice
200 ml/7 fl oz double cream

2 tsp wholegrain mustard
2 tbsp freshly chopped dill
4 tbsp vodka
salt and freshly ground

black pepper
sprigs of dill, to garnish

Bring a large pan of lightly salted water to a rolling boil. Add the pasta and cook according to the packet instructions, or until 'al dente'.

Meanwhile, cut the smoked trout into thin slivers, using scissors. Sprinkle lightly with the lemon juice and reserve.

Place the cream, mustard, chopped dill and vodka in a small pan. Season lightly with salt and pepper. Bring the contents of the pan to the boil and simmer gently for 2–3 minutes, or until slightly thickened.

Drain the cooked pasta thoroughly, then return to the pan. Add the smoked trout to the dill and vodka sauce, then pour over the pasta. Toss gently until the pasta is coated and the trout evenly mixed.

Spoon into a warmed serving dish or on to individual plates. Garnish with sprigs of dill and serve immediately.

Try This: FOR A LIGHTER OPTION: 88   FOR AN ALTERNATIVE: 216

Fish Lasagne

SERVES 4

75 g/3 oz mushrooms
1 tsp sunflower oil
1 small onion, peeled and
   finely chopped
1 tbsp freshly
   chopped oregano
400 g can chopped tomatoes
1 tbsp tomato purée
salt and freshly ground

black pepper
450 g/1 lb cod or haddock
   fillets, skinned
9–12 sheets pre-cooked
   lasagne verde

For the topping:
1 medium egg, beaten
125 g/4 oz cottage cheese

150 ml/¼ pint natural
   yoghurt
50 g/2 oz Cheddar cheese,
   grated

To serve:
mixed salad leaves
cherry tomatoes

Preheat the oven to 190°C/375°F/Gas Mark 5. Wipe the mushrooms, trim the stalks and chop. Heat the oil in a large heavy-based pan, add the onion and gently cook the onion for 3–5 minutes or until soft. Stir in the mushrooms, the oregano and the chopped tomatoes with their juice. Blend the tomato purée with 1 tablespoon of water. Stir into the pan and season to taste with salt and pepper. Bring the sauce to the boil, then simmer uncovered for 5–10 minutes.

Remove as many of the tiny pin bones as possible from the fish and cut into cubes and add to the tomato sauce mixture. Stir gently and remove the pan from the heat.

Cover the base of an ovenproof dish with 2–3 sheets of the lasagne verde. Top with half of the fish mixture. Repeat the layers finishing with the lasagne sheets.

To make the topping, mix together the beaten egg, cottage cheese and yoghurt. Pour over the lasagne and sprinkle with the cheese.

Cook the lasagne in the preheated oven for 40–45 minutes or until the topping is golden brown and bubbling. Serve the lasagne immediately with the mixed salad leaves and cherry tomatoes.

Try This: FOR A LIGHTER OPTION: 44   FOR AN ALTERNATIVE: 146

Pappardelle with Smoked Haddock & Blue Cheese Sauce

SERVES 4

350 g/12 oz smoked haddock
2 bay leaves
300 ml/½ pint milk
400 g/14 oz pappardelle
  or tagliatelle
25 g/1 oz butter
25 g/1 oz plain flour

150 ml/¼ pint single cream
  or extra milk
125 g/4 oz Dolcelatte cheese
  or Gorgonzola, cut into
  small pieces
¼ tsp freshly grated nutmeg
salt and freshly ground

black pepper
40 g/1½ oz toasted walnuts,
  chopped
1 tbsp freshly chopped
  parsley

Place the smoked haddock in a saucepan with 1 bay leaf and pour in the milk. Bring to the boil slowly, cover and simmer for 6–7 minutes, or until the fish is opaque. Remove and roughly flake the fish, discarding the skin and any bones. Strain the milk and reserve.

Bring a large pan of lightly salted water to a rolling boil. Add the pasta and cook according to the packet instructions, or until 'al dente'.

Meanwhile, place the butter, flour and single cream or milk if preferred, in a pan and stir to mix. Stir in the reserved warm milk and add the remaining bay leaf. Bring to the boil, whisking all the time until smooth and thick. Gently simmer for 3–4 minutes, stirring frequently. Discard the bay leaf.

Add the Dolcelatte or Gorgonzola cheese to the sauce. Heat gently, stirring until melted. Add the flaked haddock and season to taste with nutmeg and salt and pepper.

Drain the pasta thoroughly and return to the pan. Add the sauce and toss gently to coat, taking care not to break up the flakes of fish. Tip into a warmed serving bowl, sprinkle with toasted walnuts and parsley and serve immediately.

Try This: FOR A LIGHTER OPTION: 50 FOR AN ALTERNATIVE: 228

Smoked Haddock Rosti

SERVES 4

450 g/1 lb potatoes, peeled and coarsely grated
1 large onion, peeled and coarsely grated
2–3 garlic cloves, peeled and crushed
450 g/1 lb smoked haddock

1 tbsp olive oil
salt and freshly ground black pepper
finely grated rind of ½ lemon
1 tbsp freshly chopped parsley

2 tbsp half-fat crème fraîche
mixed salad leaves, to garnish
lemon wedges, to serve

Dry the grated potatoes in a clean tea towel. Rinse the grated onion thoroughly in cold water, dry in a clean tea towel and add to the potatoes.

Stir the garlic into the potato mixture. Skin the smoked haddock and remove as many of the tiny pin bones as possible. Cut into thin slices and reserve.

Heat the oil in a non-stick frying pan. Add half the potatoes and press well down in the frying pan. Season to taste with salt and pepper.

Add a layer of fish and a sprinkling of lemon rind, parsley and a little black pepper.

Top with the remaining potatoes and press down firmly. Cover with a sheet of tinfoil and cook on the lowest heat for 25–30 minutes.

Preheat the grill 2–3 minutes before the end of cooking time. Remove the tinfoil and place the rosti under the grill to brown. Turn out on to a warmed serving dish, and serve immediately with spoonfuls of crème fraîche, lemon wedges and mixed salad leaves.

Try This: FOR A LIGHTER OPTION: 92 FOR AN ALTERNATIVE: 144

Smoked Haddock Kedgeree

SERVES 4

450 g/1 lb smoked haddock fillets
50 g/2 oz butter
1 onion, peeled and finely chopped
2 tsp mild curry powder

175 g/6 oz long-grain rice
450 ml/¾ pint fish or vegetable stock, heated
2 large eggs, hard-boiled and shelled
2 tbsp freshly

chopped parsley
2 tbsp whipping cream (optional)
salt and freshly ground black pepper
pinch of cayenne pepper

Place the haddock in a shallow frying pan and cover with 300 ml/½ pint water. Simmer gently for 8–10 minutes, or until the fish is cooked. Drain, then remove all the skin and bones from the fish and flake into a dish. Keep warm.

Melt the butter in a saucepan and add the chopped onion and curry powder. Cook, stirring, for 3–4 minutes, or until the onion is soft, then stir in the rice. Cook for a further minute, stirring continuously, then stir in the hot stock.

Cover and simmer gently for 15 minutes, or until the rice has absorbed all the liquid. Cut the eggs into quarters or eighths and add half to the mixture with half the parsley.

Carefully fold in the cooked fish to the mixture and add the cream, if using. Season to taste with salt and pepper. Heat the kedgeree through briefly until piping hot.

Transfer the mixture to a large dish and garnish with the remaining quartered eggs, parsley and serve with a pinch of cayenne pepper. Serve immediately.

Try This: FOR A LIGHTER OPTION: 70   FOR AN ALTERNATIVE: 202

Pasta Provençale

SERVES 4

2 tbsp olive oil
1 garlic clove, peeled and
    crushed
1 onion, peeled and finely
    chopped
1 small fennel bulb, trimmed
    and halved and
    thinly sliced

400 g can chopped tomatoes
1 rosemary sprig, plus extra
    sprig to garnish
350 g/12 oz monkfish,
    skinned
2 tsp lemon juice
400 g/14 oz gnocchi pasta
50 g/2 oz pitted black olives

200 g can flageolet beans,
    drained and rinsed
1 tbsp freshly chopped
    oregano, plus sprig to
    garnish
salt and freshly ground
    black pepper

Heat the olive oil in a large saucepan, add the garlic and onion and cook gently for 5 minutes. Add the fennel and cook for a further 5 minutes. Stir in the chopped tomatoes and rosemary sprig. Half-cover the pan and simmer for 10 minutes.

Cut the monkfish into bite-sized pieces and sprinkle with the lemon juice. Add to the tomatoes, cover and simmer gently for 5 minutes, or until the fish is opaque.

Meanwhile, bring a large pan of lightly salted water to a rolling boil. Add the pasta and cook according to the packet instructions, or until 'al dente'. Drain the pasta thoroughly and return to the saucepan.

Remove the rosemary from the tomato sauce. Stir in the black olives, flageolet beans and chopped oregano, then season to taste with salt and pepper. Add the sauce to the pasta and toss gently together to coat, taking care not to break up the monkfish. Tip into a warmed serving bowl. Garnish with rosemary and oregano sprigs and serve immediately.

Try This: FOR A LIGHTER OPTION: 58   FOR AN ALTERNATIVE: 128

Warm Swordfish Niçoise

SERVES 4

4 swordfish steaks, about 2.5
  cm/1 inch thick, weighing
  about 175 g/6 oz each
juice of 1 lime
2 tbsp olive oil
salt and freshly ground
  black pepper

400 g/14 oz farfalle
225 g/8 oz French beans,
  topped and cut in half
1 tsp Dijon mustard
2 tsp white wine vinegar
pinch caster sugar
3 tbsp olive oil

225 g/8 oz ripe tomatoes,
  quartered
50 g/2 oz pitted black olives
2 medium eggs, hard boiled
  and quartered
8 anchovy fillets, drained
  and cut in half lengthways

Place the swordfish steaks in a shallow dish. Mix the lime juice with the oil, season to taste with salt and pepper and spoon over the steaks. Turn the steaks to coat them evenly. Cover and place in the refrigerator to marinate for 1 hour.

Bring a large pan of lightly salted water to a rolling boil. Add the farfalle and cook according to the packet instructions, or until 'al dente'. Add the French beans about 4 minutes before the end of cooking time.

Mix the mustard, vinegar and sugar together in a small jug. Gradually whisk in the olive oil to make a thick dressing.

Cook the swordfish in a griddle pan or under a hot preheated grill for 2 minutes on each side, or until just cooked through; overcooking will make it tough and dry. Remove and cut into 2 cm/¾ inch chunks.

Drain the pasta and beans thoroughly and place in a large bowl. Pour over the dressing and toss to coat. Add the cooked swordfish, tomatoes, olives, hard-boiled eggs and anchovy fillets. Gently toss together, taking care not to break up the eggs. Tip into a warmed serving bowl or divide the pasta between individual plates. Serve immediately.

Try This: FOR A LIGHTER OPTION: 76   FOR AN ALTERNATIVE: 126

Potato Boulangere with Sea Bass

SERVES

450 g/1 lb potatoes, peeled and thinly sliced
1 large onion, peeled and thinly sliced

salt and freshly ground black pepper
300 ml/½ pint fish or vegetable stock

75 g/3 oz butter or margarine
350 g/12 oz sea bass fillets
sprigs of fresh flat-leaf parsley, to garnish

Preheat the oven to 200°C/400°F/Gas Mark 6. Lightly grease a shallow 1.4 litre/2½ pint baking dish with oil or butter. Layer the potato slices and onions alternately in the prepared dish, seasoning each layer with salt and pepper.

Pour the stock over the top, then cut 50 g/2 oz of the butter or margarine into small pieces and dot over the top layer. Bake in the preheated oven for 50–60 minutes. Do not cover the dish at this stage.

Lightly rinse the sea bass fillets and pat dry on absorbent kitchen paper. Cook in a griddle, or heat the remaining butter or margarine in a frying pan and shallow fry the fish fillets for 3–4 minutes per side, flesh side first. Remove from the pan with a slotted spatula and drain on absorbent kitchen paper.

Remove the partly cooked potato and onion mixture from the oven and place the fish on the top. Cover with tinfoil and return to the oven for 10 minutes until heated through. Garnish with sprigs of parsley and serve immediately.

Try This: FOR A LIGHTER OPTION: 32   FOR AN ALTERNATIVE: 164

Fish Roulades
with Rice & Spinach

SERVES 4

4 x 175 g/6 oz lemon
  sole, skinned
salt and freshly ground
  black pepper
1 tsp fennel seeds
75 g/3 oz long-grain

rice, cooked
150 g/5 oz white crab meat,
  fresh or canned
125 g/4 oz baby spinach,
  washed and trimmed
5 tbsp dry white wine

5 tbsp half-fat crème fraîche
2 tbsp freshly chopped
  parsley, plus extra
  to garnish
asparagus spears,
  to serve

Wipe each fish fillet with either a clean damp cloth or kitchen paper. Place on a chopping board, skinned side up and season lightly with salt and black pepper.

Place the fennel seeds in a pestle and mortar and crush lightly. Transfer to a small bowl and stir in the cooked rice. Drain the crab meat thoroughly. Add to the rice mixture and mix lightly.

Lay 2–3 spinach leaves over each fillet and top with a quarter of the crab meat mixture. Roll up and secure with a cocktail stick if necessary. Place into a large pan and pour over the wine. Cover and cook on a medium heat for 5–7 minutes or until cooked.

Remove the fish from the cooking liquor, and transfer to a serving plate and keep warm. Stir the crème fraîche into the cooking liquor and season to taste. Heat for 3 minutes, then stir in the chopped parsley.

Spoon the sauce on to the base of a plate. Cut each roulade into slices and arrange on top of the sauce. Serve with freshly cooked asparagus spears.

Try This: FOR A LIGHTER OPTION: 46 FOR AN ALTERNATIVE: 234

Sweet-&-Sour Prawns with Noodles

SERVES 4

425 g can pineapple pieces
    in natural juice
1 green pepper, deseeded
    and cut into quarters
1 tbsp groundnut oil
1 onion, cut into thin wedges

3 tbsp soft brown sugar
150 ml/¼ pint chicken stock
4 tbsp wine vinegar
1 tbsp tomato purée
1 tbsp light soy sauce
1 tbsp cornflour

350 g/12 oz raw tiger
    prawns, peeled
225 g/8 oz pak choi, shredded
350 g/12 oz medium
    egg noodles
coriander leaves, to garnish

Drain the pineapple and reserving 2 tablespoons of the juice. Remove the membrane from the quartered peppers and cut into thin strips.

Heat the oil in a saucepan. Add the onion and pepper and cook for about 4 minutes or until the onion has softened. Add the pineapple, the sugar, stock, vinegar, tomato purée and the soy sauce.

Bring the sauce to the boil and simmer for about 4 minutes. Blend the cornflour with the reserved pineapple juice and stir into the pan, stirring until thickened.

Clean the prawns if needed. Wash the pak choi thoroughly, then shred. Add the prawns and pak choi to the sauce. Simmer gently for 3 minutes or until the prawns are cooked and have turned pink.

Cook the noodles in boiling water for 4–5 minutes until just tender. Drain and arrange the noodles on a warmed plate and pour over the sweet-and-sour prawns. Garnish with coriander leaves and serve immediately.

Try This: FOR A LIGHTER OPTION: 66   FOR AN ALTERNATIVE: 290

Louisiana Prawns & Fettuccine

SERVES 4

4 tbsp olive oil
450 g/1 lb raw tiger prawns, washed and peeled, shells and heads reserved
2 shallots, peeled and finely chopped
4 garlic cloves, peeled and finely chopped
large handful fresh

basil leaves
1 carrot, peeled and finely chopped
1 onion, peeled and finely chopped
1 celery stick, trimmed and finely chopped
2–3 sprigs fresh parsley
2–3 sprigs fresh thyme

salt and freshly ground black pepper
pinch cayenne pepper
175 ml/6 fl oz dry white wine
450 g/1 lb ripe tomatoes, roughly chopped
juice of ½ lemon, or to taste
350 g/12 oz fettuccine

Heat 2 tablespoons of the olive oil in a large saucepan and add the reserved prawn shells and heads. Fry over a high heat for 2–3 minutes. Add half the shallots, half the garlic, half the basil and the carrot, onion, celery, parsley and thyme. Season lightly with salt, pepper and cayenne and sauté for 2–3 minutes, stirring often. Pour in the wine and stir. Bring to the boil and simmer for 1 minute, then add the tomatoes. Cook for a further 3–4 minutes then pour in 200 ml/7 fl oz water. Bring to the boil, lower the heat and simmer for about 30 minutes, stirring often and using a wooden spoon to mash the prawn shells to release flavour into the sauce. Lower the heat if the sauce is reducing very quickly.

Strain through a sieve; there should be about 450 ml/¾ pint. Pour the liquid into a clean pan and bring to the boil, then lower the heat and simmer gently until the liquid is reduced by about half. Heat the remaining olive oil over a high heat in a clean frying pan and add the peeled prawns. Season lightly and add the lemon juice. Cook for 1 minute, lower the heat and add the remaining shallots and garlic. Cook for 1 minute. Add the sauce and adjust the seasoning. Meanwhile, bring a large pan of lightly salted water to a rolling boil and add the fettuccine. Cook according to the packet instructions, or until 'al dente', and drain thoroughly. Transfer to a warmed serving dish. Add the sauce and toss well. Garnish with the remaining basil and serve immediately.

Try This: FOR A LIGHTER OPTION: 62   FOR AN ALTERNATIVE: 292

Chicken & Prawn–stacked Ravioli

SERVES 4

1 tbsp olive oil
1 onion, peeled and chopped
1 garlic clove, peeled
   and chopped
450 g/1 lb boned and
   skinned cooked chicken,
   cut into large pieces

1 beefsteak tomato,
   deseeded and chopped
150 ml/¼ pint dry white wine
150 ml/¼ pint double cream
250 g/9 oz peeled cooked
   prawns, thawed if frozen
2 tbsp freshly chopped

tarragon, plus sprigs
   to garnish
salt and freshly ground
   black pepper
8 sheets fresh lasagne

Heat the olive oil in a large frying pan, add the onion and garlic and cook for 5 minutes, or until softened, stirring occasionally. Add the chicken pieces and fry for 4 minutes, or until heated through, turning occasionally.

Stir in the chopped tomato, wine and cream and bring to the boil. Lower the heat and simmer for about 5 minutes, or until reduced and thickened. Stir in the prawns and tarragon and season to taste with salt and pepper. Heat the sauce through gently.

Meanwhile, bring a large pan of lightly salted water to the boil and add 2 lasagne sheets. Return to the boil and cook for 2 minutes, stirring gently to avoid sticking. Remove from the pan using a slotted spoon and keep warm. Repeat with the remaining sheets.

Cut each sheet of lasagne in half. Place two pieces on each of the warmed plates and divide half of the chicken mixture among them. Top each serving with a second sheet of lasagne and divide the remainder of the chicken mixture among them. Top with a final layer of lasagne. Garnish with tarragon sprigs and serve immediately.

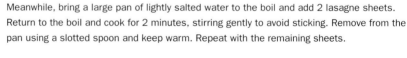

Try This: FOR A LIGHTER OPTION: 56 FOR AN ALTERNATIVE: 258

Pea & Prawn Risotto

SERVES 6

450 g/1 lb whole raw prawns
125 g/4 oz butter
1 red onion, peeled
   and chopped
4 garlic cloves, peeled and

  finely chopped
225 g/8 oz Arborio rice
150 ml/¼ pint dry white wine
1.1 litres/2 pints vegetable
  or fish stock

375 g/13 oz frozen peas
4 tbsp freshly chopped mint
salt and freshly ground
   black pepper

Peel the prawns and reserve the heads and shells. Remove the black vein from the back of each prawn, then wash and dry on absorbent kitchen paper. Melt half the butter in a large frying pan, add the prawns' heads and shells and fry, stirring occasionally for 3–4 minutes, or until golden. Strain the butter, discard the heads and shells and return the butter to the pan.

Add a further 25 g/1 oz of butter to the pan and fry the onion and garlic for 5 minutes until softened, but not coloured. Add the rice and stir the grains in the butter for 1 minute, until they are coated thoroughly. Add the white wine and boil rapidly until the wine is reduced by half.

Bring the stock to a gentle simmer, and add to the rice, a ladleful at a time. Stir constantly, adding the stock as it is absorbed, until the rice is creamy, but still has a bite in the centre.

Melt the remaining butter and stir-fry the prawns for 3–4 minutes. Stir into the rice, along with all the pan juices and the peas. Add the chopped mint and season to taste with salt and pepper. Cover the pan and leave the prawns to infuse for 5 minutes before serving.

Try This: FOR A LIGHTER OPTION: 60   FOR AN ALTERNATIVE: 296

Seafood Rice Ring

SERVES 4

350 g/12 oz long-grain rice
½ tsp turmeric
5 tbsp sunflower oil
2 tbsp white wine vinegar
1 tsp Dijon mustard
1 tsp caster sugar
1 tbsp mild curry paste

4 shallots, peeled and
    finely chopped
salt and freshly ground
    black pepper
125 g/4 oz peeled prawns,
    thawed if frozen
2 tbsp freshly chopped

    coriander
8 fresh crevettes or large tiger
    prawns, with shells on
4 sprigs of fresh coriander,
    to garnish
lemon wedges, to serve

Lightly oil a 1.1 litre/2 pint ring mould, or line the mould with clingfilm. Cook the rice in boiling salted water with the turmeric for 15 minutes, or until tender. Drain thoroughly. Whisk 4 tablespoons of the oil with the vinegar, mustard and sugar to form a dressing and pour over the warm rice. Reserve.

Heat the remaining oil in a saucepan, add the curry paste and shallots and cook for 5 minutes, or until the shallots are just softened. Fold into the dressed rice, season to taste with salt and pepper and mix well. Leave to cool completely.

Stir in the prawns and the chopped coriander and turn into the prepared ring mould. Press the mixture down firmly with a spoon, then chill in the refrigerator for at least 1 hour.

Invert the ring onto a serving plate and fill the centre with the crevettes or tiger prawns. Arrange the cooked mussels around the edge of the ring and garnish with sprigs of fresh coriander. Serve immediately with lemon wedges.

Try This: FOR A LIGHTER OPTION: 86   FOR AN ALTERNATIVE: 240

Royal Fried Rice

SERVES 4

450 g/1 lb Thai fragrant rice
2 large eggs
2 tsp sesame oil
salt and freshly ground
   black pepper
3 tbsp vegetable oil
1 red pepper, deseeded and
   finely diced
1 yellow pepper, deseeded

and finely diced
1 green pepper, deseeded
   and finely diced
2 red onions, peeled
   and diced
125 g/4 oz sweetcorn kernels
125 g/4 oz cooked peeled
   prawns, thawed if frozen
125 g/4 oz white crabmeat,

drained if canned
¼ tsp sugar
2 tsp light soy sauce

To garnish:
radish roses
freshly snipped and whole
   chive leaves

Place the rice in a sieve, rinse with cold water, then drain. Place in a saucepan and add twice the volume of water, stirring briefly. Bring to the boil, cover and simmer gently for 15 minutes without further stirring. If the rice has fully absorbed the water while covered, add a little more water. Continue to simmer, uncovered, for another 5 minutes, or until the rice is fully cooked and the water has evaporated. Leave to cool.

Place the eggs, sesame oil and a pinch of salt in a small bowl. Using a fork, mix just to break the egg. Reserve. Heat a wok and add 1 tablespoon of the vegetable oil. When very hot, stir-fry the peppers, onion and sweetcorn for 2 minutes or until the onion is soft. Remove the vegetables and reserve.

Clean the wok and add the remaining oil. When very hot, add the cold cooked rice and stir-fry for 3 minutes, or until it is heated through. Drizzle in the egg mixture and continue to stir-fry for 2–3 minutes or until the eggs have set.

Add the prawns and crabmeat to the rice. Stir-fry for 1 minute. Season to taste with salt and pepper and add the sugar with the soy sauce. Stir to mix and spoon into a warmed serving dish. Garnish with a radish flower and sprinkle with freshly snipped and whole chives. Serve immediately.

Try This: FOR A LIGHTER OPTION: 80   FOR AN ALTERNATIVE: 284

Thai Fried Rice
with Prawns & Chillies

SERVES 4

350 g/12 oz Thai fragrant rice
2 tbsp groundnut or
　vegetable oil
2 garlic cloves, peeled and
　finely chopped
2 red chillies, deseeded and
　finely chopped

125 g/4 oz peeled raw prawns
1 tbsp Thai fish sauce
¼ tsp sugar
1 tbsp light soy sauce
½ small onion, peeled and
　finely sliced
½ red pepper, deseeded and

　finely sliced
1 spring onion, green part
　only, cut into long strips
sprigs of fresh coriander,
　to garnish

Wash the rice in several changes of water until the water remains relatively clear. Drain well. Bring a large saucepan of salted water to the boil and add the rice. Cook for 12–15 minutes until tender. Drain well and reserve.

Heat a wok, add the oil and when very hot, add the garlic and stir-fry for 20 seconds, or until just browned. Add the chillies and prawns and stir-fry for 2–3 minutes.

Add the fish sauce, sugar and soy sauce and stir-fry for another 30 seconds, or until the prawns are cooked through.

Add the cooked rice to the wok and stir together well. Then add the onion, red pepper and spring onion, mix together for a further 1 minute, then turn onto a serving platter. Garnish with sprigs of fresh coriander and serve immediately.

Try This: FOR A LIGHTER OPTION: 72　FOR AN ALTERNATIVE: 314

Jambalayan–style Fried Rice

SERVES 6

450 g/1 lb long-grain rice
900 ml/1½ pints hot chicken
  or fish stock
2 fresh bay leaves
2 tbsp vegetable oil
2 medium onions, peeled
  and roughly chopped
1 green pepper, deseeded
  and roughly chopped
2 sticks celery, trimmed and

roughly chopped
3 garlic cloves, peeled and
  finely chopped
1 tsp dried oregano
300 g/11 oz skinless chicken
  breast fillets, chopped
125 g/4 oz chorizo sausage,
  chopped
3 tomatoes, peeled and
  chopped

12 large raw prawns, peeled
  if preferred
4 spring onions, trimmed
  and finely chopped
2 tbsp freshly chopped
  parsley
salt and freshly ground
  black pepper

Put the rice, stock and bay leaves into a large saucepan and bring to the boil. Cover with a tight-fitting lid and simmer for 10 minutes over a very low heat. Remove from the heat and leave for a further 10 minutes.

Meanwhile, heat a large wok, then add the oil and heat. When hot, add the onions, green pepper, celery, garlic and oregano. Stir-fry for 6 minutes, or until all the vegetables have softened. Add the chicken and chorizo and stir-fry for a further 6 minutes, or until lightly browned.

Add the tomatoes and cook over a medium heat for 2–3 minutes until collapsed. Then stir in the prawns and cook for a further 4 minutes, or until they are cooked through. Stir in the cooked rice, spring onions and chopped parsley and season to taste with salt and pepper. Serve immediately.

Try This: FOR A LIGHTER OPTION: 82   FOR AN ALTERNATIVE: 316

Creamy Mixed Seafood with Spaghetti

SERVES 4

350 g/12 oz spaghetti
2 tbsp groundnut oil
1 bunch spring onions, trimmed and diagonally sliced
1 garlic clove, peeled and chopped
125 g/4 oz frozen peas

175 g/6 oz peeled prawns, thawed if frozen
¼ cucumber, peeled if preferred and chopped
150 ml/¼ pint dry vermouth or white wine
150 ml/¼ pint double cream
420 g can salmon, drained,

boned, skinned and flaked
pinch of paprika
salt and freshly ground black pepper
50 g/2 oz freshly grated Parmesan cheese (optional)

Bring a large saucepan of salted water to the boil and add the spaghetti. Bring back to the boil and cook at a rolling boil for 8 minutes, or until 'al dente'. Drain thoroughly.

Meanwhile heat a large wok, then add the oil and heat until almost smoking. Stir-fry the spring onions for 2 minutes, then add the garlic and peas and stir-fry for 3 minutes.

Add the prawns and stir-fry for 2 minutes, until heated through and browned slightly. Add the cucumber and cook for 2 minutes.

Stir in the vermouth or white wine and bring to the boil. Simmer for 3 minutes, until reduced and thickened slightly. Add the cream, stirring until well blended, then add the salmon and paprika. Bring almost to the boil, toss in the pasta and cook until heated through. Season to taste with salt and pepper, add the Parmesan cheese, if desired, and serve immediately.

Try This: FOR A LIGHTER OPTION: 90   FOR AN ALTERNATIVE: 298

Special Seafood Lasagne

SERVES 4-6

450 g/1 lb fresh haddock
  fillet, skinned
150 ml/¼ pint dry white wine
150 ml/¼ pint fish stock
½ onion, peeled and
  thickly sliced
1 bay leaf
75 g/3 oz butter

350 g/12 oz leeks, trimmed
  and thickly sliced
1 garlic clove, peeled and
  crushed
25 g/1 oz plain flour
150 ml/¼ pint single cream
2 tbsp freshly chopped dill
salt and freshly ground

black pepper
8–12 sheets dried lasagne
  verde, cooked
225 g/8 oz ready-cooked
  seafood cocktail
50 g/2 oz Gruyère
  cheese, grated

Preheat the oven to 200°C/400°F/Gas Mark 6, 15 minutes before cooking. Place the haddock in a pan with the wine, fish stock, onion and bay leaf. Bring to the boil slowly, cover and simmer gently for 5 minutes, or until the fish is opaque. Remove and flake the fish, discarding any bones. Strain the cooking juices and reserve.

Melt 50 g/2 oz of the butter in a large saucepan. Add the leeks and garlic and cook gently for 10 minutes. Remove from the pan, using a slotted draining spoon, and reserve.

Melt the remaining butter in a small saucepan. Stir in the flour, then gradually whisk in the cream, off the heat, followed by the reserved cooking juices. Bring to the boil slowly, whisking until thickened. Stir in the dill and season to taste with salt and pepper.

Spoon a little of the sauce into the base of a buttered 2.8 litre/5 pint shallow oven-proof dish. Top with a layer of lasagne, followed by the haddock, seafood cocktail and leeks. Spoon over enough sauce to cover. Continue layering up, finishing with sheets of lasagne topped with sauce.

Sprinkle over the grated Gruyère cheese and bake in the preheated oven for 40–45 minutes, or until golden-brown and bubbling. Serve immediately.

Try This: FOR A LIGHTER OPTION: 72   FOR AN ALTERNATIVE: 300

Seafood Parcels with Pappardelle & Coriander Pesto

SERVES 4

300 g/11 oz pappardelle
or tagliatelle
8 raw tiger prawns, shelled
12 raw queen scallops
225 g/8 oz baby squid,
cleaned and cut
into rings

4 tbsp dry white wine
4 thin slices of lemon

For the coriander pesto:
50 g/2 oz fresh coriander
leaves
1 garlic clove, peeled

25 g/1 oz pine nuts, toasted
1 tsp lemon juice
5 tbsp olive oil
1 tbsp grated Parmesan
cheese
salt and freshly ground
black pepper

Preheat the oven to 180°C/350°F/Gas Mark 4, 10 minutes before cooking. To make the pesto, blend the coriander leaves, garlic, pine nuts and lemon juice with 1 tablespoon of the olive oil to a smooth paste in a food processor. With the motor running slowly add the remaining oil. Stir the Parmesan cheese into the pesto and season to taste with salt and pepper.

Bring a pan of lightly salted water to a rolling boil. Add the pasta and cook for 3 minutes only. Drain thoroughly, return to the pan and spoon over two-thirds of the pesto. Toss to coat.

Cut out 4 circles, about 30 cm/12 in in diameter, from non-stick baking parchment. Spoon the pasta on to one half of each circle. Top each pile of pasta with 2 prawns, 3 scallops and a few squid rings. Spoon 1 tablespoon of wine over each serving, then drizzle with the remaining coriander pesto and top with a slice of lemon.

Close the parcels by folding over the other half of the paper, to make a semi-circle, then turn and twist the edges of the paper to secure.

Place the parcels on a baking tray and bake in the preheated oven for 15 minutes, or until cooked. Serve the parcels immediately, allowing each person to open their own.

Creamy Coconut Seafood Pasta

SERVES 4

400 g/14 oz egg tagliatelle
1 tsp sunflower oil
1 tsp sesame oil
4 spring onions, trimmed
 and sliced diagonally
1 garlic clove, peeled
 and crushed
1 red chilli, deseeded and

finely chopped
2.5 cm/1 inch piece fresh
 root ginger, peeled
 and grated
150 ml/¼ pint coconut milk
100 ml/3½ fl oz double
 cream
225 g/8 oz cooked peeled

tiger prawns
185 g/6 oz fresh white
 crab meat
2 tbsp freshly chopped
 coriander, plus sprigs
 to garnish
salt and freshly ground
 black pepper

Bring a large pan of lightly salted water to a rolling boil. Add the pasta and cook according to the packet instructions, or until 'al dente'.

Meanwhile, heat the sunflower and sesame oils together in a saucepan. Add the spring onions, garlic, chilli and ginger and cook for 3–4 minutes, or until softened.

Blend the coconut milk and cream together in a jug. Add the prawns and crab meat to the pan and stir over a low heat for a few seconds to heat through. Gradually pour in the coconut cream, stirring all the time.

Stir the chopped coriander into the seafood sauce and season to taste with salt and pepper. Continue heating the sauce gently until piping hot, but do not allow to boil.

Drain the pasta thoroughly and return to the pan. Add the seafood sauce and gently toss together to coat the pasta. Tip into a warmed serving dish or spoon on to individual plates. Serve immediately, garnished with fresh coriander sprigs.

Try This: FOR A LIGHTER OPTION: 76   FOR AN ALTERNATIVE: 288

Paella

SERVES 4

450 g/1 lb live mussels
4 tbsp olive oil
6 medium chicken thighs
1 medium onion, peeled and
    finely chopped
1 garlic clove, peeled and
    crushed
225 g/8 oz tomatoes,
    skinned, deseeded
    and chopped

1 red pepper, deseeded
    and chopped
1 green pepper, deseeded
    and chopped
125 g/4 oz frozen peas
1 tsp paprika
450 g/1 lb Arborio rice
½ tsp turmeric
900 ml/1½ pints chicken
    stock, warmed

175 g/6 oz large
    peeled prawns
salt and freshly ground
    black pepper
2 limes
1 lemon
1 tbsp freshly chopped basil
whole cooked unpeeled
    prawns, to garnish

Rinse the mussels under cold running water, scrubbing well to remove any grit and barnacles, then pull off the hairy 'beards'. Tap any open mussels sharply with a knife, and discard if they refuse to close. Heat the oil in a paella pan or large, heavy-based frying pan and cook the chicken thighs for 10–15 minutes until golden. Remove and keep warm. Fry the onion and garlic in the remaining oil in the pan for 2–3 minutes, then add the tomatoes, peppers, peas and paprika and cook for a further 3 minutes.

Add the rice to the pan and return the chicken with the turmeric and half the stock. Bring to the boil and simmer, gradually adding more stock as it is absorbed. Cook for 20 minutes, or until most of the stock has been absorbed and the rice is almost tender.

Put the mussels in a large saucepan with 5 cm/2 inches boiling salted water, cover and steam for 5 minutes. Discard any with shells that have not opened, then stir into the rice with the prawns. Season to taste with salt and pepper. Heat through for 2–3 minutes until piping hot. Squeeze the juice from 1 of the limes over the paella. Cut the remaining limes and the lemon into wedges and arrange on top of the paella. Sprinkle with the basil, garnish with the prawns and serve.

Try This: FOR A LIGHTER OPTION: 90 FOR AN ALTERNATIVE: 312

Seafood Risotto

SERVES 4

50 g/2 oz butter
2 shallots, peeled and finely chopped
1 garlic clove, peeled and crushed
350 g/12 oz Arborio rice

150 ml/¼ pint white wine
600 ml/1 pint fish or vegetable stock, heated
125 g/4 oz large prawns
290 g can baby clams
50 g/2 oz smoked salmon

trimmings
2 tbsp freshly chopped parsley

To serve:
green salad
crusty bread

Melt the butter in a large, heavy-based saucepan, add the shallots and garlic and cook for 2 minutes until slightly softened. Add the rice and cook for 1–2 minutes, stirring continuously, then pour in the wine and boil for 1 minute.

Pour in half the hot stock, bring to the boil, cover the saucepan and simmer gently for 15 minutes, adding the remaining stock a little at a time. Continue to simmer for 5 minutes, or until the rice is cooked and all the liquid is absorbed.

Meanwhile, prepare the fish by peeling the prawns and removing the heads and tails. Drain the clams and discard the liquid. Cut the smoked salmon trimmings into thin strips.

When the rice has cooked, stir in the prawns, clams, smoked salmon strips and half the chopped parsley, then heat through for 1–2 minutes until everything is piping hot. Turn into a serving dish, sprinkle with the remaining parsley and the Parmesan cheese and serve immediately with a green salad and crusty bread.

Try This: FOR A LIGHTER OPTION: 72   FOR AN ALTERNATIVE: 300

Linguine with Fennel, Crab & Chervil

SERVES 6

450 g/1 lb linguine
25 g/1 oz butter
2 carrots, peeled and
    finely diced
2 shallots, peeled and
    finely diced
2 celery sticks, trimmed and

finely diced
1 bulb fennel, trimmed and
    finely diced
6 spring onions, trimmed
    and finely chopped
300 ml/½ pint double cream
3 tbsp freshly chopped chervil

1 large cooked crab plus
    extra for garnish
salt and freshly ground
    pepper
juice of ½ lemon, or to taste
sprig of dill, to garnish

Bring a large pan of lightly salted water to a rolling boil. Add the pasta and cook according to the packet instructions, or until 'al dente'.

Meanwhile, heat the butter in a large saucepan. Add the carrots, shallots, celery, fennel and three-quarters of the chopped spring onions. Cook the vegetables gently for 8–10 minutes, or until tender, stirring frequently and ensuring that they do not brown.

Add the double cream and chopped chervil to the vegetable mixture. Scrape the crab meat over the sauce, then stir to mix the sauce ingredients.

Season the sauce to taste with salt and pepper and stir in the lemon juice. Drain the pasta thoroughly and transfer to a large warmed serving dish. Pour over the sauce and toss. Garnish with extra chervil, the remaining spring onions and a sprig of dill. Serve immediately.

Try This: FOR A LIGHTER OPTION: 76   FOR AN ALTERNATIVE: 246

Conchiglioni with Crab au Gratin

SERVES 4

175 g/6 oz large pasta shells
50 g/2 oz butter
1 shallot, peeled and finely chopped
1 bird's-eye chilli, deseeded and finely chopped
2 x 200 g cans crabmeat, drained

3 tbsp plain flour
50 ml/2 fl oz white wine
50 ml/2 fl oz milk
3 tbsp crème fraîche
15 g/½ oz Cheddar cheese, grated
salt and freshly ground black pepper

1 tbsp oil or melted butter
50 g/2 oz fresh white breadcrumbs

To serve:
cheese or tomato sauce
tossed green salad or freshly cooked baby vegetables

Preheat the oven to 200°C/400°F/Gas Mark 6, 15 minutes before cooking. Bring a large pan of lightly salted water to a rolling boil. Add the pasta shells and cook according to the packet instructions, or until 'al dente'. Drain thoroughly and allow to dry completely.

Melt half the butter in a heavy-based pan, add the shallots and chilli and cook for 2 minutes, then stir in the crabmeat. Stuff the cooled shells with the crab mixture and reserve.

Melt the remaining butter in a small pan and stir in the flour. Cook for 1 minute, then whisk in the wine and milk and cook, stirring, until thickened. Stir in the crème fraîche and grated cheese and season the sauce to taste with salt and pepper.

Place the crab filled shells in a lightly oiled, large shallow baking dish or tray and spoon a little of the sauce over. Toss the breadcrumbs in the melted butter or oil, then sprinkle over the pasta shells. Bake in the preheated oven for 10 minutes. Serve immediately with a cheese or tomato sauce and a tossed green salad or cooked baby vegetables.

Try This: FOR A LIGHTER OPTION: 80   FOR AN ALTERNATIVE: 266

Spaghetti alle Vongole

SERVES 4

1.8 kg/4 lb small fresh clams
6 tbsp dry white wine
2 tbsp olive oil
1 small onion, peeled and
  finely chopped

2 garlic cloves, peeled
  and crushed
400 g/14 oz spaghetti
2 tbsp freshly chopped parsley
2 tbsp freshly chopped or

torn basil
salt and freshly ground
  black pepper
oregano leaves, to garnish

Soak the clams in lightly salted cold water for 8 hours before required, changing the water once or twice. Scrub the clams, removing any that have broken shells or that remain open when tapped.

Place the prepared clams in a large saucepan and pour in the wine. Cover with a tight-fitting lid and cook over a medium heat for 5–6 minutes, shaking the pan occasionally, until the shells have opened.

Strain the clams and cooking juices through a sieve lined with muslin and reserve. Discard any clams that have remained unopened.

Heat the olive oil in a saucepan and fry the onion and garlic gently for 10 minutes, or until very soft.

Meanwhile, bring a large pan of lightly salted water to a rolling boil. Add the spaghetti and cook according to the packet instructions, or until 'al dente'.

Add the cooked clams to the onions and garlic and pour in the reserved cooking juices. Bring to the boil, then add the parsley and basil and season to taste with salt and black pepper.

Drain the spaghetti thoroughly. Return to the pan and add the clams with their sauce. Toss together gently, then tip into a large warmed serving bowl or into individual bowls. Serve immediately, sprinkled with oregano leaves.

Try This: FOR A LIGHTER OPTION: 48 FOR AN ALTERNATIVE: 138

Red Pesto & Clam Spaghetti

SERVES 4

For the red pesto:
2 garlic cloves, peeled and finely chopped
50 g/2 oz pine nuts
25 g/1 oz fresh basil leaves
4 sun-dried tomatoes in oil, drained
4 tbsp olive oil
4 tbsp Parmesan cheese, grated
salt and freshly ground black pepper

For the clam sauce:
450 g/1 lb live clams, in their shells
1 tbsp olive oil
2 garlic cloves, peeled and crushed
1 small onion, peeled and chopped
5 tbsp medium dry white wine
150 ml/¼ pint fish or chicken stock
275 g/10 oz spaghetti

To make the red pesto, place the garlic, pine nuts, basil leaves, sun-dried tomatoes and olive oil in a food processor and blend in short, sharp bursts until smooth. Scrape into a bowl, then stir in the Parmesan cheese and season to taste with salt and pepper. Cover and leave in the refrigerator until required.

Scrub the clams with a soft brush and remove any beards from the shells, discard any shells that are open or damaged. Wash in plenty of cold water then leave in a bowl covered with cold water in the refrigerator until required. Change the water frequently.

Heat the olive oil in a large saucepan and gently fry the garlic and onion for 5 minutes until softened, but not coloured. Add the wine and stock and bring to the boil. Add the clams, cover and cook for 3–4 minutes, or until the clams have opened.

Discard any clams that have not opened and stir in the red pesto sauce. Bring a large saucepan of lightly salted water to the boil and cook the spaghetti for 5–7 minutes, or until 'al dente'. Drain and return to the saucepan. Add the sauce to the spaghetti, mix well, then spoon into a serving dish and serve immediately.

Try This: FOR A LIGHTER OPTION: 56   FOR AN ALTERNATIVE: 186

Pasta & Mussels in Tomato & Wine Sauce

SERVES 4

900 g/2 lb fresh live mussels
1 bay leaf
150 ml/¼ pint light red wine
15 g/½ oz unsalted butter
1 tbsp olive oil
1 red onion, peeled and
   thinly sliced

2 garlic cloves, peeled
   and crushed
550 g/1¼ lb ripe tomatoes,
   skinned, deseeded and
   chopped
400 g/14 oz fiochetti
   or penne

3 tbsp freshly chopped
   or torn basil
salt and freshly ground
   black pepper
basil leaves, to garnish
crusty bread, to serve

Scrub the mussels and remove any beards. Discard any that do not close when lightly tapped. Place in a large pan with the bay leaf and pour in the wine. Cover with a tight-fitting lid and steam, shaking the pan occasionally, for 3–4 minutes, or until the mussels open. Remove the mussels with a slotted spoon, discarding any that have not opened, and reserve. Strain the cooking liquid through a muslin-lined sieve and reserve.

Melt the butter with the oil in a large saucepan and gently cook the onion and garlic for 10 minutes, until soft. Add the reserved cooking liquid and the tomatoes and simmer, uncovered, for 6–7 minutes, or until very soft and the sauce has reduced slightly.

Meanwhile, bring a large pan of lightly salted water to a rolling boil. Add the pasta and cook acording to the packet instructions, or until 'al dente'.

Drain the pasta thoroughly and return to the pan. Add the mussels, removing the shells if you prefer, with the tomato sauce. Stir in the basil and season to taste with salt and pepper. Toss together gently. Tip into warmed serving bowls, garnish with basil leaves and serve with crusty bread.

Try This: FOR A LIGHTER OPTION: 76   FOR AN ALTERNATIVE: 146

Mussels Linguine

SERVES 4

2 kg/4½ lb fresh mussels,
    washed and scrubbed
knob of butter
1 onion, peeled and
    finely chopped
300 ml/½ pint medium dry
    white wine

For the sauce:
1 tbsp sunflower oil
4 baby onions, peeled
    and quartered
2 garlic cloves, peeled
    and crushed
400 g can chopped tomatoes

large pinch of salt
225 g/8 oz dried linguine
    or tagliatelle
2 tbsp freshly chopped
    parsley

Soak the mussels in plenty of cold water. Leave in the refrigerator until required. When ready to use, scrub the mussel shells, removing any barnacles or beards. Discard any open mussels.

Melt the butter in a large pan. Add the mussels, onion and wine. Cover with a close-fitting lid and steam for 5–6 minutes, shaking the pan gently to ensure even cooking. Discard any mussels that have not opened, then strain and reserve the liquor.

To make the sauce, heat the oil in a medium-sized saucepan, and gently fry the quartered onion and garlic for 3–4 minutes until soft and transparent. Stir in the tomatoes and half the reserved mussel liquor. Bring to the boil and simmer for 7–10 minutes until the sauce begins to thicken.

Cook the pasta in boiling salted water for 7 minutes or or until 'al dente'. Drain the pasta, reserving 2 tablespoons of the cooking liquor, then return the pasta and liquor to the pan.

Remove the meat from half the mussel shells. Stir into the sauce along with the remaining mussels. Pour the hot sauce over the cooked pasta and toss gently. Garnish with the parsley and serve immediately.

Try This: FOR A LIGHTER OPTION: 90   FOR AN ALTERNATIVE: 176

Spaghetti with Hot Chilli Mussels

SERVES 4

900 g/2 lb fresh live mussels
300 ml/½ pint white wine
3–4 garlic cloves, peeled
    and crushed
2 tbsp olive oil
1–2 bird's-eye chillies,

deseeded and chopped
2 x 400 g cans chopped
    tomatoes
salt and freshly ground
    black pepper
350 g/12 oz fresh spaghetti

2 tbsp freshly chopped
    parsley, to garnish
warm crusty bread,
    to serve

Scrub the mussels and remove any beards. Discard any that do not close when tapped. Place in a large pan with the white wine and half the crushed garlic. Cover and cook over a high heat for 5–6 minutes, shaking the pan from time to time. When the mussels have opened, drain, reserving the juices and straining them through a muslin-lined sieve. Discard any mussels that have not opened and keep the rest warm.

Heat the oil in a heavy-based pan, add the remaining garlic with the chillies and cook for 30 seconds. Stir in the chopped tomatoes and 75 ml/3 fl oz of the reserved cooking liquor and simmer for 15–20 minutes. Season to taste with salt and pepper.

Meanwhile, bring a large pan of lightly salted water to a rolling boil. Add the spaghetti and cook according to the packet instructions, about 3–4 minutes, or until 'al dente'.

Drain the spaghetti thoroughly and return to the pan. Add the mussels and tomato sauce to the pasta, toss lightly to cover, then tip into a warmed serving dish or spoon on to individual plates. Garnish with chopped parsley and serve immediately with warm crusty bread.

Try This: FOR A LIGHTER OPTION: 86   FOR AN ALTERNATIVE: 312

Pan–fried Scallops & Pasta

SERVES 4

16 large scallops, shelled
1 tbsp olive oil
1 garlic clove, peeled
  and crushed
1 tsp freshly chopped thyme
400 g/14 oz penne
4 sun-dried tomatoes in oil,
  drained and thinly sliced

thyme or oregano sprigs,
  to garnish

For the tomato dressing:
2 sun-dried tomatoes in oil,
  drained and chopped
1 tbsp red wine vinegar
2 tsp balsamic vinegar

1 tsp sun-dried tomato paste
1 tsp caster sugar
salt and freshly ground
  black pepper
2 tbsp oil from a jar of
  sun-dried tomatoes
2 tbsp olive oil

Rinse the scallops and pat dry on absorbent kitchen paper. Place in a bowl and add the olive oil, crushed garlic and thyme. Cover and chill in the refrigerator until ready to cook.

Bring a large pan of lightly salted water to a rolling boil. Add the penne and cook according to the packet instructions, or until 'al dente'.

Meanwhile, make the dressing. Place the sun-dried tomatoes into a small bowl or glass jar and add the vinegars, tomato paste, sugar, salt and pepper. Whisk well, then pour into a food processor. With the motor running, pour in the sun-dried tomato oil and olive oil in a steady stream to make a thick, smooth dressing.

Preheat a large, dry cast-iron griddle pan over a high heat for about 5 minutes. Lower the heat to medium then add the scallops to the pan. Cook for 1½ minutes on each side. Remove from the pan.

Drain the pasta thoroughly and return to the pan. Add the sliced sun-dried tomatoes and dressing and toss. Divide between individual serving plates, top each portion with 4 scallops, garnish with fresh thyme or oregano sprigs and serve immediately.

Try This: FOR A LIGHTER OPTION: 82   FOR AN ALTERNATIVE: 316

Squid & Prawns with Saffron Rice

SERVES 4

2 tbsp groundnut oil
1 large onion, peeled and
    sliced
2 garlic cloves, peeled and
    chopped
450 g/1 lb tomatoes,
    skinned, deseeded and
    chopped
225 g/8 oz long-grain rice

¼ tsp saffron strands
600 ml/1 pint fish stock
225 g/8 oz firm fish fillets,
    such as monkfish or cod
225 g/8 oz squid, cleaned
225 g/8 oz mussels with shells
75 g/3 oz frozen or shelled
    fresh peas
225 g/8 oz peeled prawns,

    thawed if frozen
salt and freshly ground
    black pepper

To garnish:
8 whole cooked prawns
lemon wedges

Heat a large wok, add the oil and when hot, stir-fry the onion and garlic for 3 minutes. Add the tomatoes and continue to stir-fry for 1 minute before adding the rice, saffron and stock. Bring to the boil, reduce the heat, cover and simmer for 10 minutes, stirring occasionally.

Meanwhile, remove any skin from the fish fillets, rinse lightly and cut into small cubes. Rinse the squid, pat dry with absorbent kitchen paper, then cut into rings and reserve. Scrub the mussels, discarding any that stay open after being tapped on the work surface. Cover with cold water and reserve until required.

Add the peas to the wok together with the fish and return to a gentle simmer. Cover and simmer for 5–10 minutes, or until the rice is tender and most of the liquid has been absorbed.

Uncover and stir in the squid, the drained prepared mussels and the peeled prawns. Re-cover and simmer for 5 minutes, or until the mussels have opened. Discard any unopened ones. Season to taste with salt and pepper. Garnish with whole cooked prawns and lemon wedges, then serve immediately.

Try This: FOR A LIGHTER OPTION: 52   FOR AN ALTERNATIVE: 322

Baked, Grilled, Seared, Steamed & Poached

Zesty Whole–baked Fish

SERVES 8

1.8 kg/4 lb whole salmon, cleaned
sea salt and freshly ground black pepper
50 g/2 oz margarine
1 garlic clove, peeled and finely sliced

zest and juice of 1 lemon
zest of 1 orange
1 tsp freshly grated nutmeg
3 tbsp Dijon mustard
2 tbsp fresh white breadcrumbs
2 bunches fresh dill

1 bunch fresh tarragon
1 lime sliced
150 ml/¼ pint crème fraîche
450 ml/¾ pint fromage frais
dill sprigs, to garnish

Preheat the oven to 220°C/425°F/Gas Mark 7. Lightly rinse the fish and pat dry with absorbent kitchen paper. Season the cavity with a little salt and pepper. Make several diagonal cuts across the flesh of the fish and season.

Mix together the margarine, garlic, lemon and orange zest and juice, nutmeg, mustard and fresh breadcrumbs. Mix well together. Spoon the breadcrumb mixture into the slits with a small sprig of dill. Place the remaining herbs inside the fish cavity. Weigh the fish and calculate the cooking time. Allow 10 minutes per 450 g/1 lb.

Lay the fish on double thickness tinfoil. If liked, smear the fish with a little low fat spread. Top with the lime slices and fold the foil into a parcel. Chill in the refrigerator for about 15 minutes.

Place in a roasting tin and cook in the preheated oven for the calculated cooking time. Fifteen minutes before the end of cooking, open the foil and return until the skin begins to crisp. Remove the fish from the oven and stand for 10 minutes.

Pour the juices from the roasting tin into a saucepan. Bring to the boil and stir in the crème fraîche and fromage frais. Simmer for 3 minutes or until hot. Garnish with dill sprigs and serve immediately.

Try This: FOR A LIGHTER OPTION: 74 FOR AN ALTERNATIVE: 318

Salmon Teriyaki with Noodles & Crispy Greens

SERVES 4

350 g/12 oz salmon fillet
3 tbsp Japanese soy sauce
3 tbsp mirin or sweet sherry
3 tbsp sake
1 tbsp freshly grated
   root ginger

225 g/8 oz spring greens
groundnut oil for
   deep-frying
pinch of salt
½ tsp caster sugar
125 g/4 oz cellophane noodles

To garnish:
1 tbsp freshly chopped dill
sprigs of fresh dill
zest of ½ lemon

Cut the salmon into paper-thin slices and place in a shallow dish. Mix together the soy sauce, mirin or sherry, sake and the ginger. Pour over the salmon, cover and leave to marinate for 15–30 minutes.

Remove and discard the thick stalks from the spring greens. Lay several leaves on top of each other, roll up tightly, then shred finely. Pour in enough oil to cover about 5 cm/2 inches of the wok. Deep-fry the greens in batches for about 1 minute each until crisp. Remove and drain on kitchen paper. Transfer to a serving dish, sprinkle with salt and sugar and toss together.

Place the noodles in a bowl and pour over warm water to cover. Leave to soak for 15–20 minutes until soft, then drain. With scissors cut into 15 cm/6 inch lengths.

Preheat the grill. Remove the salmon slices from the marinade, reserving the marinade for later, and arrange them in a single layer on a baking sheet. Grill for about 2 minutes, until lightly cooked, without turning.

When the oil in the wok is cool enough, tip most of it away, leaving about 1 tablespoon behind. Heat until hot, then add the noodles and the reserved marinade and stir-fry for 3–4 minutes. Tip the noodles into a bowl and arrange the salmon slices on top, garnished with chopped dill, sprigs of fresh dill, lemon zest and a little of the crispy greens. Serve with the crispy greens.

Try This: FOR A LIGHTER OPTION: 24 FOR AN ALTERNATIVE: 106

Seared Tuna with Pernod & Thyme

SERVES 4

4 tuna or swordfish steaks
salt and freshly ground
   black pepper
3 tbsp Pernod

1 tbsp olive oil
zest and juice of 1 lime
2 tsp fresh thyme leaves
4 sun-dried tomatoes

To serve:
freshly cooked mixed rice
tossed green salad

Wipe the fish steaks with a damp cloth or dampened kitchen paper.

Season both sides of the fish to taste with salt and pepper, then place in a shallow bowl and reserve.

Mix together the Pernod, olive oil, lime zest and juice with the fresh thyme leaves. Finely chop the sun-dried tomatoes and add to the Pernod mixture.

Pour the Pernod mixture over the fish and chill in the refrigerator for about 2 hours, spooning the marinade occasionally over the fish.

Heat a griddle or heavy-based frying pan. Drain the fish, reserving the marinade. Cook the fish for 3–4 minutes on each side for a steak that is still slightly pink in the middle. Or, if liked, cook the fish for 1–2 minutes longer on each side if you prefer your fish cooked through.

Place the remaining marinade in a small saucepan and bring to the boil. Pour the marinade over the fish and serve immediately, with the mixed rice and salad.

Try This: FOR A LIGHTER OPTION: 40   FOR AN ALTERNATIVE: 120

Seared Tuna
with Italian Salsa

SERVES 4

4 x 175 g/6 oz tuna or
   swordfish steaks
salt and freshly ground
   black pepper
3 tbsp Pernod
2 tbsp olive oil
zest and juice of 1 lemon
2 tsp fresh thyme leaves
2 tsp fennel seeds, lightly
   roasted

4 sun-dried tomatoes,
   chopped
1 tsp dried chilli flakes
assorted salad leaves,
   to serve

For the salsa:
1 white onion, peeled and
   finely chopped
2 tomatoes, deseeded

and sliced
2 tbsp freshly shredded
   basil leaves
1 red chilli, deseeded and
   finely sliced
3 tbsp extra-virgin olive oil
2 tsp balsamic vinegar
1 tsp caster sugar

Wipe the fish and season lightly with salt and pepper, then place in a shallow dish. Mix together the Pernod, olive oil, lemon zest and juice, thyme, fennel seeds, sun-dried tomatoes and chilli flakes and pour over the fish. Cover lightly and leave to marinate in a cool place for 1–2 hours, occasionally spooning the marinade over the fish.

Meanwhile, mix all the ingredients for the salsa together in a small bowl. Season to taste with salt and pepper, then cover and leave for about 30 minutes to allow all the flavours to develop.

Lightly oil a griddle pan and heat until hot. When the pan is very hot, drain the fish, reserving the marinade. Cook the fish for 3–4 minutes on each side, taking care not to overcook them – the tuna steaks should be a little pink inside. Pour any remaining marinade into a small saucepan, bring to the boil and boil for 1 minute. Serve the steaks hot with the marinade, chilled salsa and a few assorted salad leaves.

Try This: FOR A LIGHTER OPTION: 38   FOR AN ALTERNATIVE: 122

Barbecued Fish Kebabs

SERVES 4

450 g/1 lb herring
or mackerel fillets, cut
into chunks
2 small red onions, peeled
and quartered
16 cherry tomatoes

salt and freshly ground
black pepper

For the sauce:
150 ml/¼ pint fish stock
5 tbsp tomato ketchup

2 tbsp Worcestershire sauce
2 tbsp wine vinegar
2 tbsp brown sugar
2 drops Tabasco
2 tbsp tomato purée

Line a grill rack with a single layer of tinfoil and preheat the grill at a high temperature, 2 minutes before use.

If using wooden skewers, soak in cold water for 30 minutes to prevent them from catching alight during cooking.

Meanwhile, prepare the sauce. Add the fish stock, tomato ketchup, Worcestershire sauce, vinegar, sugar, Tabasco and tomato purée to a small saucepan. Stir well and leave to simmer for 5 minutes.

When ready to cook, drain the skewers, if necessary, then thread the fish chunks, the quartered red onions and the cherry tomatoes alternately on to the skewers.

Season the kebabs to taste with salt and pepper and brush with the sauce. Grill under the preheated grill for 8–10 minutes, basting with the sauce occasionally during cooking. Turn the kebabs often to ensure that they are cooked thoroughly and evenly on all sides. Serve immediately with couscous.

Try This: FOR A LIGHTER OPTION: 88   FOR AN ALTERNATIVE: 248

Grilled Red Mullet
with Orange & Anchovy Sauce

SERVES 4

2 oranges
4 x 175 g/6 oz red mullet,
   cleaned and descaled
salt and freshly ground
   black pepper
4 sprigs of fresh rosemary

1 lemon, sliced
2 tbsp olive oil
2 garlic cloves, peeled
   and crushed
6 anchovy fillets in oil,
   drained and roughly

   chopped
2 tsp freshly chopped
   rosemary
1 tsp lemon juice

Preheat the grill and line the grill rack with tinfoil just before cooking. Peel the oranges with a sharp knife, over a bowl in order to catch the juice. Cut into thin slices and reserve. If necessary, make up the juice to 150 ml/¼ pint with extra juice.

Place the fish on a chopping board and make 2 diagonal slashes across the thickest part of both sides of the fish. Season well, both inside and out, with salt and pepper. Tuck a rosemary sprig and a few lemon slices inside the cavity of each fish. Brush the fish with a little of the olive oil and then cook under the preheated grill for 4–5 minutes on each side. The flesh should just fall away from the bone.

Heat the remaining oil in a saucepan and gently fry the garlic and anchovies for 3–4 minutes. Do not allow to brown. Add the chopped rosemary and plenty of black pepper. The anchovies will be salty enough, so do not add any salt. Stir in the orange slices with their juice and the lemon juice. Simmer gently until heated through. Spoon the sauce over the red mullet and serve immediately.

Try This: FOR A LIGHTER OPTION: 34   FOR AN ALTERNATIVE: 234

Grilled Snapper with Roasted Pepper

SERVES 4

1 medium red pepper
1 medium green pepper
4–8 snapper fillets, depending on size, about 450 g/1 lb

sea salt and freshly ground black pepper
1 tbsp olive oil
5 tbsp double cream
125 ml/4 fl oz white wine

1 tbsp freshly chopped dill
sprigs of fresh dill, to garnish
freshly cooked tagliatelle, to serve

Preheat the grill to a high heat and line the grill rack with tinfoil. Cut the tops off the peppers and divide into quarters. Remove the seeds and the membrane, then place on the foil-lined grill rack and cook for 8–10 minutes, turning frequently, until the skins have become charred and blackened. Remove from the grill rack, place in a polythene bag and leave until cool. When the peppers are cool, strip off the skin, slice thinly and reserve.

Cover the grill rack with another piece of tinfoil, then place the snapper fillets skin-side up on the grill rack. Season to taste with salt and pepper and brush with a little of the olive oil. Cook for 10–12 minutes, turning over once and brushing again with a little olive oil.

Pour the cream and wine into a small saucepan, bring to the boil and simmer for about 5 minutes until the sauce has thickened slightly. Add the dill, season to taste and stir in the sliced peppers. Arrange the cooked snapper fillets on warm serving plates and pour over the cream and pepper sauce. Garnish with sprigs of dill and serve immediately with freshly cooked tagliatelle.

Try This: FOR A LIGHTER OPTION: 50   FOR AN ALTERNATIVE: 136

Steamed Whole Trout with Ginger & Spring Onion

SERVES 4

2 x 450–700 g/1–1½ lb whole
  trout, gutted with heads
  removed
coarse sea salt
2 tbsp groundnut oil
½ tbsp soy sauce
1 tbsp sesame oil

2 garlic cloves, peeled and
  thinly sliced
2.5 cm/1 inch piece fresh
  root ginger, peeled and
  thinly slivered
2 spring onions, trimmed
  and thinly sliced diagonally

To garnish:
chive leaves
lemon slices

To serve:
freshly cooked rice
Oriental salad, to serve

Wipe the fish inside and out with absorbent kitchen paper then rub with salt inside and out and leave for about 20 minutes. Pat dry with absorbent kitchen paper.

Set a steamer rack or inverted ramekin in a large wok and pour in enough water to come about 5 cm/2 inches up the side of the wok. Bring to the boil.

Brush a heatproof dinner plate with a little of the groundnut oil and place the fish on the plate with the tails pointing in opposite directions. Place the plate on the rack, cover tightly and simmer over a medium heat for 10–12 minutes, or until tender and the flesh is opaque near the bone.

Carefully transfer the plate to a heatproof surface. Sprinkle with the soy sauce and keep warm.

Pour the water out of the wok and return to the heat. Add the remaining groundnut and sesame oils and when hot, add the garlic, ginger and spring onion and stir-fry for 2 minutes, or until golden. Pour over the fish, garnish with chive leaves and lemon slices and serve immediately with rice and an Oriental salad.

Try This: FOR A LIGHTER OPTION: 34 FOR AN ALTERNATIVE: 152

Sardines with Redcurrants

SERVES 4

2 tbsp redcurrant jelly
finely grated rind of 1 lime
2 tbsp medium dry sherry
450 g /1 lb fresh sardines,
   cleaned and heads

removed
sea salt and freshly ground
   black pepper
lime wedges, to garnish

To serve:
fresh redcurrants
fresh green salad

Preheat the grill and line the grill rack with tinfoil 2–3 minutes before cooking.

Warm the redcurrant jelly in a bowl standing over a pan of gently simmering water and stir until smooth. Add the lime rind and sherry to the bowl and stir well until blended.

Lightly rinse the sardines and pat dry with absorbent kitchen paper.

Place on a chopping board and with a sharp knife make several diagonal cuts across the flesh of each fish. Season the sardines inside the cavities with salt and pepper.

Gently brush the warm marinade over the skin and inside the cavities of the sardines. Place on the grill rack and cook under the preheated grill for 8–10 minutes, or until the fish are cooked.

Carefully turn the sardines over at least once during grilling. Baste occasionally with the remaining redcurrant and lime marinade. Garnish with the redcurrants. Serve immediately with the salad and lime wedges.

Try This: FOR A LIGHTER OPTION: 66   FOR AN ALTERNATIVE: 270

Seared
Pancetta–wrapped Cod

SERVES 4

4 x 175 g/6 oz thick cod fillets
4 very thin slices of pancetta
3 tbsp capers in vinegar
1 tbsp of vegetable or
   sunflower oil

2 tbsp lemon juice
1 tbsp olive oil
freshly ground
   black pepper
1 tbsp freshly chopped

parsley, to garnish

To serve:
freshly cooked vegetables
new potatoes

Wipe the cod fillets and wrap each one with the pancetta. Secure each fillet with a cocktail stick and reserve.

Drain the capers and soak in cold water for 10 minutes to remove any excess salt, then drain and reserve.

Heat the oil in a large frying pan and sear the wrapped pieces of cod fillet for about 3 minutes on each side, turning carefully with a fish slice so as not to break up the fish. Lower the heat then continue to cook for 2–3 minutes or until the fish is cooked thoroughly.

Meanwhile, place the reserved capers, lemon juice and olive oil into a small saucepan. Grind over the black pepper.

Place the saucepan over a low heat and bring to a gentle simmer, stirring continuously for 2–3 minutes.

Once the fish is cooked, garnish with the parsley and serve with the warm caper dressing, freshly cooked vegetables and new potatoes.

Try This: FOR A LIGHTER OPTION: 90   FOR AN ALTERNATIVE: 130

Gingered Cod Steaks

SERVES 4

2.5 cm/1 inch piece fresh
    root ginger, peeled
4 spring onions
2 tsp freshly chopped

parsley
1 tbsp soft brown sugar
4 x 175 g/6 oz thick cod steaks
salt and freshly ground

black pepper
25 g/1 oz butter
freshly cooked vegetables,
    to serve

Preheat the grill and line the grill rack with a layer of tinfoil. Coarsely grate the piece of ginger. Trim the spring onions and cut into thin strips.

Mix the spring onions, ginger, chopped parsley and sugar. Add 1 tablespoon of water.

Wipe the fish steaks. Season to taste with salt and pepper. Place on to 4 separate 20.5 x 20.5 cm/8 x 8 inch tinfoil squares.

Carefully spoon the spring onions and ginger mixture over the fish. Cut the butter into small cubes and place over the fish.

Loosely fold the foil over the steaks to enclose the fish and to make a parcel. Place under the preheated grill and cook for 10–12 minutes or until cooked and the flesh has turned opaque.

Place the fish parcels on individual serving plates. Serve immediately with the freshly cooked vegetables.

Try This: FOR A LIGHTER OPTION: 62 FOR AN ALTERNATIVE: 134

Cod with Fennel & Cardamom

SERVES 4

1 garlic clove, peeled
 and crushed
finely grated rind of 1 lemon
1 tsp lemon juice

1 tbsp olive oil
1 fennel bulb
1 tbsp cardamom pods
salt and freshly ground

black pepper
4 x 175 g/6 oz thick
 cod fillets

Preheat the oven to 190°C/375°F/Gas Mark 5. Place the garlic in a small bowl with the lemon rind, juice and olive oil and stir well. Cover and leave to infuse for at least 30 minutes. Stir well before using.

Trim the fennel bulb, thinly slice and place in a bowl.

Place the cardamom pods in a pestle and mortar and lightly pound to crack the pods. Alternatively place in a polythene bag and pound gently with a rolling pin. Add the crushed cardamom to the fennel slices.

Season the fish with salt and pepper and place on to 4 separate 20.5 x 20.5 cm/8 x 8 inch parchment paper squares.

Spoon the fennel mixture over the fish and drizzle with the infused oil. Place the parcels on a baking sheet and bake in the preheated oven for 8–10 minutes or until cooked. Serve immediately in the paper parcels.

Try This: FOR A LIGHTER OPTION: 58 FOR AN ALTERNATIVE: 226

Roasted Cod
with Saffron Aïoli

SERVES 4

For the saffron aïoli:
2 garlic cloves, peeled
¼ tsp saffron strands
sea salt, to taste
1 medium egg yolk
200 ml/7 fl oz extra-virgin
    olive oil
2 tbsp lemon juice

For the marinade:
2 tbsp olive oil
4 garlic cloves, peeled and
    finely chopped
1 red onion, peeled and
    finely chopped
1 tbsp freshly chopped
    rosemary

2 tbsp freshly chopped
    thyme
4–6 sprigs of fresh rosemary
1 lemon, sliced
4 x 175 g/6 oz thick cod
    fillets with skin
freshly cooked vegtables,
    to serve

Preheat oven to 180°C/350°F/Gas Mark 4, 10 minutes before cooking. Crush the garlic, saffron and a pinch of salt in a pestle and mortar to form a paste. Place in a blender with the egg yolk and blend for 30 seconds. With the motor running, slowly add the olive oil in a thin, steady stream until the mayonnaise is smooth and thick. Spoon into a small bowl and stir in the lemon juice. Cover and leave in the refrigerator until required.

Combine the olive oil, garlic, red onion, rosemary and thyme for the marinade and leave to infuse for about 10 minutes.

Place the sprigs of rosemary and slices of lemon in the bottom of a lightly oiled roasting tin. Add the cod, skinned-side up. Pour over the prepared marinade and leave to marinate in the refrigerator for 15–20 minutes. Bake in the preheated oven for 15–20 minutes, or until the cod is cooked and the flesh flakes easily with a fork. Leave the cod to rest for 1 minute before serving with the saffron aïoli and vegetables.

Try This: FOR A LIGHTER OPTION: 50 FOR AN ALTERNATIVE: 132

Haddock with an Olive Crust

SERVES 4

12 pitted black olives, finely chopped
75 g/3 oz fresh white breadcrumbs
1 tbsp freshly chopped tarragon

1 garlic clove, peeled and crushed
3 spring onions, trimmed and finely chopped
1 tbsp olive oil

4 x 175 g/6 oz thick skinless haddock fillets

To serve:
freshly cooked carrots
freshly cooked beans

Preheat the oven to 190°C/375°F/Gas Mark 5. Place the black olives in a small bowl with the breadcrumbs and add the chopped tarragon.

Add the garlic to the olives with the chopped spring onions and the olive oil. Mix together lightly.

Wipe the fillets with either a clean damp cloth or damp kitchen paper, then place on a lightly oiled baking sheet.

Place spoonfuls of the olive and breadcrumb mixture on top of each fillet and press the mixture down lightly and evenly over the top of the fish.

Bake the fish in the preheated oven for 20–25 minutes or until the fish is cooked thoroughly and the topping is golden brown. Serve immediately with the freshly cooked carrots and beans.

Try This: FOR A LIGHTER OPTION: 86   FOR AN ALTERNATIVE: 142

Fish Balls in Hot Yellow Bean Sauce

SERVES 4

450 g/1 lb skinless white fish
  fillets, such as cod or
  haddock, cut into pieces
½ tsp salt
1 tbsp cornflour
2 spring onions, trimmed
  and chopped
1 tbsp freshly chopped
  coriander

1 tsp soy sauce
1 medium egg white
freshly ground black pepper
sprig of tarragon, to garnish
freshly cooked rice, to serve

For the yellow bean sauce:
75 ml/3 fl oz fish or
  chicken stock

1–2 tsp yellow bean sauce
2 tbsp soy sauce
1–2 tbsp Chinese rice wine
  or dry sherry
1 tsp chilli bean sauce,
  or to taste
1 tsp sesame oil
1 tsp sugar (optional)

Put the fish pieces, salt, cornflour, spring onions, coriander, soy sauce and egg white into a food processor, season to taste with pepper, then blend until a smooth paste forms, scraping down the sides of the bowl occasionally.

With dampened hands, shape the mixture into 2.5 cm/1 inch balls. Transfer to a baking tray and chill in the refrigerator for at least 30 minutes.

Bring a large saucepan of water to simmering point. Working in 2 or 3 batches, drop in the fish balls and poach gently for 3–4 minutes or until they float to the top. Transfer to absorbent kitchen paper to drain.

Put all the sauce ingredients in a wok or large frying pan and bring to the boil. Add the fish balls to the sauce and stir-fry gently for 2–3 minutes until piping hot. Transfer to a warmed serving dish, garnish with sprigs of tarragon and serve immediately with freshly cooked rice.

Try This: FOR A LIGHTER OPTION: 26   FOR AN ALTERNATIVE: 210

Foil-baked Fish

SERVES 4

For the tomato sauce:
125 ml/4 fl oz olive oil
4 garlic cloves, peeled and finely chopped
4 shallots, peeled and finely chopped
400 g can chopped Italian tomatoes

2 tbsp freshly chopped flat-leaf parsley
3 tbsp basil leaves
salt and freshly ground black pepper

700 g/1½ lb red mullet, bass or haddock fillets

450 g/1 lb live mussels
4 squids
8 large raw prawns
2 tbsp olive oil
3 tbsp dry white wine
3 tbsp freshly chopped basil leaves
lemon wedges, to garnish

Preheat oven to 180°C/350°F/Gas Mark 4, 10 minutes before cooking. Heat the olive oil and gently fry the garlic and shallots for 2 minutes. Stir in the tomatoes and simmer for 10 minutes, breaking the tomatoes down with the wooden spoon. Add the parsley and basil, season to taste with salt and pepper and cook for a further 2 minutes. Reserve and keep warm.

Lightly rinse the fish fillets and cut into 4 portions. Scrub the mussels thoroughly, removing the beard and any barnacles from the shells. Discard any mussels that are open. Clean the squid and cut into rings. Peel the prawns and remove the thin black intestinal vein that runs down the back.

Cut 4 large pieces of tinfoil, then place them on a large baking sheet and brush with olive oil. Place 1 fish portion in the centre of each piece of tinfoil. Close the tinfoil to form parcels and bake in the preheated oven for 10 minutes, then remove.

Carefully open up the parcels and add the mussels, squid and prawns. Pour in the wine and spoon over a little of the tomato sauce. Sprinkle with the basil leaves and return to the oven and bake for 5 minutes, or until cooked thoroughly. Disgard any unopened mussels, then garnish with lemon wedges and serve with the extra tomato sauce.

Try This: FOR A LIGHTER OPTION: 46   FOR AN ALTERNATIVE: 344

Plaice with
Parmesan & Anchovies

SERVES 4

4 plaice fillets
4 anchovy fillets,
  finely chopped
450 g/1 lb spinach, rinsed

3 firm tomatoes, sliced
200 ml/7 fl oz double cream
5 slices of olive ciabatta bread
50 g/2 oz wild rocket

8 tbsp Parmesan
  cheese, grated
freshly cooked pasta,
  to serve

Preheat oven to 220°C/425°F/Gas Mark 7, 15 minutes before cooking. Put the plaice on a chopping board and holding the tail, strip off the skin from both sides. With a filleting knife, fillet the fish, then wipe and reserve.

Place the fillets on a large chopping board, skinned-side up and halve lengthways along the centre. Dot each one with some of the chopped anchovies, then roll up from the thickest end and reserve.

Pour boiling water over the spinach, leave for 2 minutes, drain, squeezing out as much moisture as possible, then place in the base of an ovenproof dish. Arrange the tomatoes on top of the spinach. Arrange the rolled-up fillets standing up in the dish and pour over the cream.

Place the ciabatta and rocket in a food processor and blend until finely chopped, then stir in the grated Parmesan cheese.

Sprinkle the topping over the fish and bake in the preheated oven for 8–10 minutes, or until the fish is cooked and has lost its translucency and the topping is golden brown. Serve with freshly cooked pasta.

Try This: FOR A LIGHTER OPTION: 92   FOR AN ALTERNATIVE: 334

Citrus–grilled Plaice

SERVES 4

1 tsp sunflower oil
1 onion, peeled
    and chopped
1 orange pepper, deseeded
    and chopped
175 g/6 oz long-grain rice
150 ml/¼ pint orange juice

2 tbsp lemon juice
225 ml/8 fl oz vegetable stock
spray of oil
4 x 175 g/6 oz plaice
    fillets, skinned
1 orange
1 lemon

25 g/1 oz butter or
    margarine
2 tbsp freshly
    chopped tarragon
salt and freshly ground
    black pepper
lemon wedges, to garnish

Heat the oil in a large frying pan, then sauté the onion, pepper and rice for 2 minutes.

Add the orange and lemon juice and bring to the boil. Reduce the heat, add half the stock and simmer for 15–20 minutes, or until the rice is tender, adding the remaining stock as necessary.

Preheat the grill. Finely spray the base of the grill pan with oil. Place the plaice fillets in the base and reserve.

Finely grate the orange and lemon rind. Squeeze the juice from half of each fruit.

Melt the butter or margarine in a small saucepan. Add the grated rind, juice and half of the tarragon and use to baste the plaice fillets.

Cook one side only of the fish under the preheated grill at a medium heat for 4–6 minutes, basting continuously.

Once the rice is cooked, stir in the remaining tarragon and season to taste with salt and pepper. Garnish the fish with the lemon wedges and serve immediately with the rice

Try This: FOR A LIGHTER OPTION: 34 FOR AN ALTERNATIVE: 320

Sole with Red Wine Sauce

SERVES 4

4 tbsp groundnut oil
125 g/4 oz rindless smoked streaky bacon, diced
175 g/6 oz shallots, peeled and chopped
225 g/8 oz button mushrooms, wiped
1 tbsp plain flour

2 tbsp brandy
300 ml/½ pint red wine
1 bouquet garni
1 garlic clove, peeled and chopped
salt and freshly ground black pepper
8 sole fillets, skinned and cut in half
sprigs of fresh parsley, to garnish

To serve:
freshly cooked noodles
mangetout peas

Heat a large wok, add the oil and heat. When almost smoking, stir-fry the bacon and shallots for 4–5 minutes, or until golden. Using a slotted spoon remove from the wok and keep warm. Add the mushrooms and stir-fry for 2 minutes, then remove and reserve.

Sprinkle the flour into the wok and carefully stir-fry over a medium heat for 30 seconds. Remove the wok from the heat, then return the bacon and shallots to the wok together with the brandy.

Stir in the red wine, bouquet garni, garlic and season to taste with salt and pepper. Return to the heat and bring back to the boil, stirring until smooth, then simmer for about 5 minutes, until the sauce is thickened.

Meanwhile, roll the sole fillets up and secure with either fine twine or cocktail sticks. Carefully add the rolled-up sole fillets and reserved mushrooms with seasoning to the wok. Reduce the heat, cover with a lid or tinfoil and simmer for a further 8–10 minutes, or until the fish is tender. Discard the bouquet garni, garnish with sprigs of fresh parsley and serve immediately with freshly cooked noodles and steamed mangetout peas.

Try This: FOR A LIGHTER OPTION: 28 FOR AN ALTERNATIVE: 240

Hot Salsa–filled Sole

SERVES 4

8 x 175 g/6 oz lemon
   sole fillets, skinned
150 ml/¼ pint orange juice
2 tbsp lemon juice

For the salsa:
1 small mango

8 cherry tomatoes,
   quartered
1 small red onion, peeled
   and finely chopped
pinch of sugar
1 red chilli
2 tbsp rice vinegar

zest and juice of 1 lime
1 tbsp olive oil
sea salt and freshly ground
   black pepper
2 tbsp freshly chopped mint
lime wedges, to garnish
salad leaves, to serve

First make the salsa. Peel the mango and cut the flesh away from the stone. Chop finely and place in a small bowl. Add the cherry tomatoes to the mango together with the onion and sugar.

Cut the top of the chilli. Slit down the side and discard the seeds and the membrane (the skin to which the seeds are attached). Finely chop the chilli and add to the mango mixture with the vinegar, lime zest, juice and oil. Season to taste with salt and pepper. Mix thoroughly and leave to stand for 30 minutes to allow the flavours to develop.

Lay the fish fillets on a board skinned-side up and pile the salsa on the tail end of the fillets. Fold the fillets in half, season and place in a large shallow frying pan. Pour over the orange and lemon juice.

Bring to a gentle boil, then reduce the heat to a simmer. Cover and cook on a low heat for 7–10 minutes, adding a little water if the liquid is evaporating. Remove the cover, add the mint and cook uncovered for a further 3 minutes. Garnish with lime wedges and serve immediately with the salad.

Try This: FOR A LIGHTER OPTION: 82   FOR AN ALTERNATIVE: 320

Sea Bass in Creamy
Watercress & Prosciutto Sauce

SERVES 4

75 g/3 oz watercress
450 ml/¾ pint fish or
   chicken stock
150 ml/¼ pint dry white wine
225 g/8 oz tagliatelle pasta

40 g/1½ oz butter
75 g/3 oz prosciutto ham
2 tbsp plain flour
300 ml/½ pint single cream
salt and freshly ground

black pepper
olive oil, for spraying
4 x 175 g/6 oz sea bass fillets
fresh watercress, to garnish

Remove the leaves from the watercress stalks and reserve. Chop the stalks roughly and put in a large pan with the stock. Bring to the boil slowly, cover, and simmer for 20 minutes. Strain, and discard the stalks. Make the stock up to 300 ml/½ pint with the wine.

Bring a large saucepan of lightly salted water to the boil and cook the pasta for 8–10 minutes or until 'al dente'. Drain and reserve.

Melt the butter in a saucepan, and cook the prosciutto gently for 3 minutes. Remove with a slotted spoon. Stir the flour into the saucepan and cook on a medium heat for 2 minutes. Remove from the heat and gradually pour in the hot watercress stock, stirring continuously. Return to the heat and bring to the boil, stirring throughout. Simmer for 3 minutes, or until the sauce has thickened and is smooth. Purée the watercress leaves and cream in a food processor then add to the sauce with the prosciutto. Season to taste with salt and pepper, add the pasta, toss lightly and keep warm.

Meanwhile, spray a griddle pan lightly with olive oil, then heat until hot. When hot, cook the fillets for 3–4 minutes on each side, or until cooked. Arrange the sea bass on a bed of pasta and drizzle with a little sauce. Garnish with watercress and serve immediately.

Chinese Steamed Sea Bass with Black Beans

SERVES 4

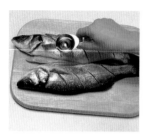

1.1 kg/2½ lb sea bass, cleaned with head and tail left on
1–2 tbsp rice wine or dry sherry
1½ tbsp groundnut oil
2–3 tbsp fermented black beans, rinsed and drained

1 garlic clove, peeled and finely chopped
1 cm/½ inch piece fresh root ginger, peeled and finely chopped
4 spring onions, trimmed and thinly sliced diagonally

2–3 tbsp soy sauce
125 ml/4 fl oz fish or chicken stock
1–2 tbsp sweet Chinese chilli sauce, or to taste
2 tsp sesame oil
sprigs of fresh coriander, to garnish

Using a sharp knife, cut 3–4 deep diagonal slashes along both sides of the fish. Sprinkle the Chinese rice wine or sherry inside and over the fish and gently rub into the skin on both sides.

Lightly brush a heatproof plate large enough to fit into a large wok or frying pan with a little of the groundnut oil. Place the fish on the plate, curving the fish along the inside edge of the dish, then leave for 20 minutes.

Place a wire rack or inverted ramekin in the wok and pour in enough water to come about 2.5 cm/1 inch up the side. Bring to the boil over a high heat. Carefully place the plate with the fish on the rack or ramekin, cover and steam for 12–15 minutes, or until the fish is tender and the flesh is opaque when pierced with a knife near the bone. Remove the plate with the fish from the wok and keep warm. Remove the rack or ramekin from the wok and pour off the water.

Return the wok to the heat, add the remaining groundnut oil and swirl to coat the bottom and side. Add the black beans, garlic and ginger and stir-fry for 1 minute. Add the spring onions, soy sauce, fish or chicken stock and boil for 1 minute. Stir in the chilli sauce and sesame oil, then pour the sauce over the cooked fish. Garnish with coriander sprigs and serve immediately.

Try This: FOR A LIGHTER OPTION: 76   FOR AN ALTERNATIVE: 110

Lime–baked Fish

SERVES 4

1 kg/2 lb 4 oz white fish
  fillets, such as bass, plaice
  or cod
1 lime, halved
3 tbsp extra-virgin olive oil

1 large onion, finely chopped
3 garlic cloves, finely
  chopped
2–3 pickled jalapeño
  chillies, chopped

6–8 tbsp chopped fresh
  coriander
salt and pepper
lemon and lime wedges,
  to serve

Place the fish fillets in a bowl and sprinkle with salt and pepper. Squeeze the juice from the lime over the fish.

Heat the olive oil in a frying pan. Add the onion and garlic and fry for about 2 minutes, stirring frequently, until softened. Remove from the heat.

Place a third of the onion mixture and a little of the chillies and coriander in the bottom of a shallow baking dish or roasting tin. Arrange the fish on top. Top with the remaining onion mixture, chillies and coriander.

Bake in a preheated oven at 180°C/350°F/Gas Mark 4 for about 15–20 minutes or until the fish has become slightly opaque and firm to the touch. Serve at once, with lemon and lime wedges for squeezing over the fish.

Try This: FOR A LIGHTER OPTION: 44   FOR AN ALTERNATIVE: 102

Fish Crumble

SERVES 6

450 g/1 lb whiting or halibut
   fillets
300 ml/½ pint milk
salt and freshly ground
   black pepper
1 tbsp sunflower oil
75 g/3 oz butter or
   margarine
1 medium onion, peeled and
   finely chopped

2 leeks, trimmed and sliced
1 medium carrot, peeled and
   cut into small dice
2 medium potatoes, peeled
   and cut into small pieces
175 g/6 oz plain flour
300 ml/½ pint fish or
   vegetable stock
2 tbsp whipping cream
1 tsp freshly chopped dill

runner beans, to serve

For the crumble topping:
75 g/3 oz butter or
   margarine
175 g/6 oz plain flour
75 g/3 oz Parmesan
   cheese, grated
¾ tsp cayenne pepper

Preheat the oven to 200°C/400°F/Gas Mark 6, 15 minutes before cooking. Oil a 1.4 litre/2½ pint pie dish. Place the fish in a saucepan with the milk, salt and pepper. Bring to the boil, cover and simmer for 8–10 minutes until the fish is cooked. Remove with a slotted spoon, reserving the cooking liquid. Flake the fish into the prepared dish.

Heat the oil and 1 tablespoon of the butter or margarine in a small frying pan and gently fry the onion, leeks, carrot and potatoes for 1–2 minutes. Cover tightly and cook over a gentle heat for a further 10 minutes until softened. Spoon the vegetables over the fish.

Melt the remaining butter or margarine in a saucepan, add the flour and cook for 1 minute, stirring. Whisk in the reserved cooking liquid and the stock. Cook until thickened, then stir in the cream. Remove from the heat and stir in the dill. Pour over the fish.

To make the crumble, rub the butter or margarine into the flour until it resembles bread-crumbs, then stir in the cheese and cayenne pepper. Sprinkle over the dish, and bake in the preheated oven for 20 minutes until piping hot. Serve with runner beans.

Try This: FOR A LIGHTER OPTION: 48   FOR AN ALTERNATIVE: 328

Roasted Monkfish with Parma Ham

SERVES 4

700 g/1½ lb monkfish tail
sea salt and freshly ground
  black pepper
4 bay leaves
4 slices fontina cheese,
  rind removed

8 slices Parma ham
225 g/8 oz angel hair pasta
50 g/2 oz butter
the zest and juice of 1 lemon
sprigs of fresh coriander,
  to garnish

To serve:
chargrilled courgettes
chargrilled tomatoes

Preheat oven to 200°C/400°F/Gas Mark 6, 15 minutes before cooking. Discard any skin from the monkfish tail and cut away and discard the central bone. Cut the fish into 4 equal-sized pieces and season to taste with salt and pepper and lay a bay leaf on each fillet, along with a slice of cheese.

Wrap each fillet with 2 slices of the Parma ham, so that the fish is covered completely. Tuck the ends of the Parma ham in and secure with a cocktail stick.

Lightly oil a baking sheet and place in the preheated oven for a few minutes. Place the fish on the preheated baking sheet, then place in the oven and cook for 12–15 minutes.

Bring a large saucepan of lightly salted water to the boil, then slowly add the pasta and cook for 5 minutes until 'al dente', or according to packet directions. Drain, reserving 2 tablespoons of the pasta-cooking liquor. Return the pasta to the saucepan and add the reserved pasta liquor, butter, lemon zest and juice. Toss until the pasta is well coated and glistening.

Twirl the pasta into small nests on 4 warmed serving plates and top with the monkfish parcels. Garnish with sprigs of coriander and serve with chargrilled courgettes and tomatoes.

Try This: FOR A LIGHTER OPTION: 76   FOR AN ALTERNATIVE: 256

Steamed Monkfish with Chilli & Ginger

SERVES 4

700 g/1½ lb skinless
  monkfish tail
1–2 red chillies
4 cm/1½ inch piece fresh
  root ginger
1 tsp sesame oil

4 spring onions, trimmed
  and thinly sliced
  diagonally
2 tbsp soy sauce
2 tbsp Chinese rice wine or
  dry sherry

freshly steamed rice,
  to serve

To garnish:
sprigs of fresh coriander
lime wedges

Place the monkfish on a chopping board. Using a sharp knife, cut down each side of the central bone and remove. Cut the fish into 2.5cm/1 inch pieces and reserve.

Make a slit down the side of each chilli, remove and discard the seeds and the membrane, then slice thinly. Peel the ginger and either chop finely or grate.

Brush a large heatproof plate with the sesame oil and arrange the monkfish pieces in one layer on the plate. Sprinkle over the spring onions and pour over the soy sauce and Chinese rice wine or sherry.

Place a wire rack or inverted ramekin in a large wok. Pour in enough water to come about 2.5 cm/1 inch up the side of the wok and bring to the boil over a high heat. Fold a long piece of tinfoil lengthways to about 5–7.5 cm/2–3 inches wide and lay it over the rack or ramekin. It must extend beyond the plate edge when it is placed in the wok.

Place the plate with the monkfish on the rack or ramekin and cover tightly. Steam over a medium-low heat for 5 minutes, or until the fish is tender and opaque. Using the tinfoil as a hammock, lift out the plate. Garnish with sprigs of coriander and lime wedges and serve immediately with steamed rice.

Try This: FOR A LIGHTER OPTION: 44   FOR AN ALTERNATIVE: 282

Citrus Monkfish Kebabs

SERVES 4

For the marinade:
1 tbsp sunflower oil
finely grated rind and juice
   of 1 lime
1 tbsp lemon juice
1 sprig of freshly

chopped rosemary
1 tbsp whole-grain mustard
1 garlic clove, peeled
   and crushed
salt and freshly ground
   black pepper

For the kebabs:
450 g/1 lb monkfish tail
8 raw tiger prawns
1 small green courgette,
   trimmed and sliced
4 tbsp of crème fraîche

Preheat the grill and line the grill rack with tinfoil. Mix all the marinade ingredients together in a small bowl and reserve.

Using a sharp knife, cut down both sides of the monkfish tail. Remove the bone and discard. Cut away and discard any skin, then cut the monkfish into bite-sized cubes.

Peel the prawns, leaving the tails intact and remove the thin black vein that runs down the back of each prawn. Place the fish and prawns in a shallow dish.

Pour the marinade over the fish and prawns. Cover lightly and leave to marinate in the refrigerator for 30 minutes. Spoon the marinade over the fish and prawns occasionally during this time. Soak the skewers in cold water for 30 minutes, then drain.

Thread the cubes of fish, prawns and courgettes on to the drained skewers.

Arrange on the grill rack then place under the preheated grill and cook for 5–7 minutes, or until cooked thoroughly and the prawns have turned pink. Occasionally brush with the remaining marinade and turn the kebabs during cooking.

Mix 2 tablespoons of the marinade with the crème fraîche and serve as a dip with the kebabs.

Try This: FOR A LIGHTER OPTION: 72   FOR AN ALTERNATIVE: 210

Scallops & Monkfish Kebabs with Fennel Sauce

SERVES 4

700 g/1½lb monkfish tail
8 large fresh scallops
2 tbsp olive oil
1 garlic clove, peeled
  and crushed
freshly ground black pepper

1 fennel bulb, trimmed and
  thinly sliced
assorted salad leaves, to serve

For the sauce:
2 tbsp fennel seeds

pinch of chilli flakes
4 tbsp olive oil
2 tsp lemon juice
salt and freshly ground
  black pepper

Place the monkfish on a chopping board and remove the skin and the bone that runs down the centre of the tail and discard. Lightly rinse and pat dry. Cut the 2 fillets into 12 equal-sized pieces and place in a shallow bowl. Remove the scallops from their shells, if necessary, and clean thoroughly discarding the black vein. Rinse lightly and pat dry. Put in the bowl with the fish.

Blend the 2 tablespoons of olive oil, the crushed garlic and a pinch of black pepper in a small bowl, then pour the mixture over the monkfish and scallops, making sure they are well coated. Cover lightly and leave to marinate in the refrigerator for at least 30 minutes, or longer if time permits. Spoon over the marinade occasionally.

Lightly crush the fennel seeds and chilli flakes in a pestle and mortar. Stir in the 4 tablespoons of olive oil and lemon juice and season to taste with salt and pepper. Cover and leave to infuse for 20 minutes.

Drain the monkfish and scallops, reserving the marinade and thread on to 4 skewers. Spray a griddle pan with a fine spray of oil, then heat until almost smoking and cook the kebabs for 5–6 minutes, turning halfway through and brushing with the marinade throughout. Brush the fennel slices with the fennel sauce and cook on the griddle for 1 minute on each side. Serve the fennel slices, topped with the kebabs and drizzled with the fennel sauce. Serve with a few assorted salad leaves.

Try This: FOR A LIGHTER OPTION: 50   FOR AN ALTERNATIVE: 316

Cheesy Vegetable & Prawn Bake

SERVES 4

175 g/6 oz long-grain rice
salt and freshly ground
  black pepper
1 garlic clove, peeled
  and crushed
1 large egg, beaten
3 tbsp freshly shredded basil

4 tbsp Parmesan cheese,
  grated
125 g/4 oz baby asparagus
  spears, trimmed
150 g/5 oz baby carrots,
  trimmed
150 g/5 oz fine green

  beans, trimmed
150 g/5 oz cherry tomatoes
175 g/6 oz peeled prawns,
  thawed if frozen
125 g/4 oz mozzarella
  cheese, thinly sliced

Preheat the oven to 200°C/400°F/Gas Mark 6, about 10 minutes before required. Cook the rice in lightly salted boiling water for 12–15 minutes, or until tender, drain. Stir in the garlic, beaten egg, shredded basil, 2 tablespoons of the Parmesan cheese and season to taste with salt and pepper. Press this mixture into a greased 23 cm/9 inch square ovenproof dish and reserve.

Bring a large saucepan of water to the boil, then drop in the asparagus, carrots and green beans. Return to the boil and cook for 3–4 minutes. Drain and leave to cool.

Quarter or halve the cherry tomatoes and mix them into the cooled vegetables. Spread the prepared vegetables over the rice and top with the prawns. Season to taste with salt and pepper.

Cover the prawns with the mozzarella and sprinkle over the remaining Parmesan cheese. Bake in the preheated oven for 20–25 minutes until piping hot and golden brown in places. Serve immediately.

Try This: FOR A LIGHTER OPTION: 70 FOR AN ALTERNATIVE: 154

Mussels with Creamy Garlic & Saffron Sauce

SERVES 4

700 g/1½ lb fresh live mussels
300 ml/½ pint good-quality dry white wine
1 tbsp olive oil
1 shallot, peeled and finely chopped
2 garlic cloves, peeled and crushed
1 tbsp freshly chopped oregano
2 saffron strands
150 ml/¼ pint single cream
salt and freshly ground black pepper
fresh crusty bread, to serve

Clean the mussels thoroughly in plenty of cold water and remove any beards and barnacles from the shells. Discard any mussels that are open or damaged. Place in a large bowl and cover with cold water and leave in the refrigerator until required, if prepared earlier.

Pour the wine into a large saucepan and bring to the boil. Tip the mussels into the pan, cover and cook, shaking the saucepan periodically for 6–8 minutes, or until the mussels have opened completely.

Discard any mussels with closed shells, then using a slotted spoon, carefully remove the remaining open mussels from the saucepan and keep them warm. Reserve the cooking liquor.

Heat the olive oil in a small frying pan and cook the shallot and garlic gently for 2–3 minutes, until softened. Add the reserved cooking liquid and chopped oregano and cook for a further 3–4 minutes. Stir in the saffron and the cream and heat through gently. Season to taste with salt and pepper. Place a few mussels in individual serving bowls and spoon over the saffron sauce. Serve immediately with plenty of fresh crusty bread.

Try This: FOR A LIGHTER OPTION: 68   FOR AN ALTERNATIVE: 310

Stuffed Squid
with Romesco Sauce

SERVES 4

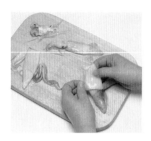

8 small squid, about
    350 g/12 oz
5 tbsp olive oil
50 g/2 oz pancetta, diced
1 onion, peeled and
    chopped
3 garlic cloves, peeled and
    finely chopped
2 tsp freshly chopped thyme

50 g/2 oz sun-dried
    tomatoes in oil drained,
    and chopped
75 g/3 oz fresh white
    breadcrumbs
2 tbsp freshly chopped basil
juice of ½ lime
salt and freshly ground
    black pepper

2 vine-ripened tomatoes,
    peeled and finely
    chopped
pinch of dried chilli flakes
1 tsp dried oregano
1 large red pepper, skinned
    and chopped
assorted salad leaves,
    to serve

Preheat oven to 230°C/450°F/Gas Mark 8, 15 minutes before cooking. Clean the squid if necessary, rinse lightly, pat dry with absorbent kitchen paper and finely chop the tentacles.

Heat 2 tablespoons of the olive oil in a large non-stick frying pan and fry the pancetta for 5 minutes, or until crisp. Remove the pancetta and reserve. Add the tentacles, onion, 2 garlic cloves, thyme and sun-dried tomatoes to the oil remaining in the pan and cook gently for 5 minutes, or until softened.

Remove the pan from the heat and stir in the diced pancetta. Blend in a food processor if a smoother stuffing is preferred, then stir in the breadcrumbs, basil and lime juice. Season to taste with salt and pepper and reserve. Spoon the stuffing into the cavity of the squid and secure the tops with cocktail sticks. Place the squid in a large roasting tin, and sprinkle over 2 tablespoons each of oil and water. Place in the preheated oven and cook for 20 minutes.

Heat the remaining oil in a saucepan and cook the remaining garlic for 3 minutes. Add the tomatoes, chilli flakes and oregano and simmer gently for 15 minutes before stirring in the red pepper. Cook gently for a further 5 minutes. Blend in a food processor to make a smooth sauce and season to taste. Pour the sauce over the squid and serve immediately with some assorted salad leaves.

Try This: FOR A LIGHTER OPTION: 88   FOR AN ALTERNATIVE: 322

Griddled Garlic & Lemon Squid

SERVES 4

125 g/4 oz long-grain rice
300 ml/½ pint fish stock
225 g/8 oz squid, cleaned
finely grated rind of 1 lemon
1 garlic clove, peeled

and crushed
1 shallot, peeled and finely chopped
2 tbsp freshly chopped coriander

2 tbsp lemon juice
salt and freshly ground black pepper

Rinse the rice until the water runs clear, then place in a saucepan with the stock. Bring to the boil, then reduce the heat. Cover and simmer gently for 10 minutes. Turn off the heat and leave the pan covered so the rice can steam while you cook the squid.

Remove the tentacles from the squid and reserve. Cut the body cavity in half. Using the tip of a small sharp knife, score the inside flesh of the body cavity in a diamond pattern. Do not cut all the way through.

Mix the lemon rind, crushed garlic and chopped shallot together.

Place the squid in a shallow bowl and sprinkle over the lemon mixture and stir. Heat a griddle pan until almost smoking. Cook the squid for 3–4 minutes until cooked through, then slice.

Sprinkle with the coriander and lemon juice. Season to taste with salt and pepper. Drain the rice and serve immediately with the squid.

Try This: FOR A LIGHTER OPTION: 36 FOR AN ALTERNATIVE: 334

Parmesan & Garlic Lobster

SERVES 2

1 large cooked lobster
25 g/1 oz unsalted butter
4 garlic cloves, peeled
    and crushed

1 tbsp plain flour
300 ml/½ pint milk
125 g/4 oz Parmesan
    cheese, grated

sea salt and freshly ground
    black pepper
assorted salad leaves,
    to serve

Preheat oven to 180°C/350°F/Gas Mark 4, 10 minutes before cooking. Halve the lobster and crack the claws. Remove the gills, green sac behind the head and the black vein running down the body. Place the 2 lobster halves in a shallow ovenproof dish.

Melt the butter in a small saucepan and gently cook the garlic for 3 minutes, until softened. Add the flour and stir over a medium heat for 1 minute. Draw the saucepan off the heat then gradually stir in the milk, stirring until the sauce thickens. Return to the heat and cook for 2 minutes, stirring throughout until smooth and thickened. Stir in half the cheese and continue to cook for 1 minute, then season to taste with salt and pepper.

Pour the cheese sauce over the lobster halves and sprinkle with the remaining Parmesan cheese. Bake in the preheated oven for 20 minutes, or until heated through and the cheese sauce is golden brown. Serve with assorted salad leaves.

Try This: FOR A LIGHTER OPTION: 84   FOR AN ALTERNATIVE: 296

Curries, Stews & Stir-fries

Salmon Noisettes with Fruity Sauce

SERVES 4

4 x 125 g/4 oz salmon steaks
grated rind and juice of 2
    lemons
grated rind and juice
    of 1 lime
3 tbsp olive oil

1 tbsp clear honey
1 tbsp wholegrain mustard
coarse sea salt and freshly
    ground black pepper
1 tbsp groundnut oil
125 g/4 oz mixed salad

leaves, washed
1 bunch watercress,
    washed and thick stalks
    removed
250 g/9 oz baby plum
    tomatoes, halved

Using a sharp knife, cut the bone away from each salmon steak to create 2 salmon fillets. Repeat with the remaining salmon steaks. Shape the salmon fillets into noisettes and secure with fine string.

Mix together the citrus rinds and juices, olive oil, honey, wholegrain mustard, salt and pepper in a shallow dish. Add the salmon fillets and turn to coat. Cover and leave to marinate in the refrigerator for 4 hours, turning them occasionally in the marinade.

Heat the wok then add the groundnut oil and heat until hot. Lift out the salmon noisettes, reserving the marinade. Add the salmon to the wok and cook for 6–10 minutes, turning once during cooking, until cooked and the fish is just flaking. Pour the marinade into the wok and heat through gently.

Mix together the salad leaves, watercress and tomatoes and arrange on serving plates. Top with the salmon noisettes and drizzle over any remaining warm marinade. Serve immediately.

Try This: FOR A LIGHTER OPTION: 24   FOR AN ALTERNATIVE: 102

Stir-fried Salmon with Peas

SERVES 4

450 g/1 lb salmon fillet
salt
6 slices streaky bacon
1 tbsp vegetable oil
50 ml/2 fl oz chicken or
   fish stock

2 tbsp dark soy sauce
2 tbsp Chinese rice wine or
   dry sherry
1 tsp sugar
75 g/3 oz frozen peas, thawed
1–2 tbsp freshly

   shredded mint
1 tsp cornflour
sprigs of fresh mint,
   to garnish
freshly cooked noodles,
   to serve

Wipe and skin the salmon fillet and remove any pin bones. Slice into 2.5 cm/1 inch strips, place on a plate and sprinkle with salt. Leave for 20 minutes, then pat dry with absorbent kitchen paper and reserve.

Remove any cartilage from the bacon, cut into small dice and reserve.

Heat a wok or large frying pan over a high heat, then add the oil and, when hot, add the bacon and stir-fry for 3 minutes or until crisp and golden. Push to one side and add the strips of salmon. Stir-fry gently for 2 minutes or until the flesh is opaque.

Pour the chicken or fish stock, soy sauce and Chinese rice wine or sherry into the wok, then stir in the sugar, peas and freshly shredded mint.

Blend the cornflour with 1 tablespoon of water to form a smooth paste and stir into the sauce. Bring to the boil, reduce the heat and simmer for 1 minute, or until slightly thickened and smooth. Garnish and serve immediately with noodles.

Try This: FOR A LIGHTER OPTION: 28   FOR AN ALTERNATIVE: 204

Teriyaki Salmon

SERVES 4

450 g/1 lb salmon
   fillet, skinned
6 tbsp Japanese teriyaki sauce
1 tbsp rice wine vinegar
1 tbsp tomato paste

dash of Tabasco sauce
grated zest of ½ lemon
salt and freshly ground
   black pepper
4 tbsp groundnut oil

1 carrot, peeled and cut into
   matchsticks
125 g/4 oz mangetout peas
125 g/4 oz oyster
   mushrooms, wiped

Using a sharp knife, cut the salmon into thick slices and place in a shallow dish. Mix together the teriyaki sauce, rice wine vinegar, tomato paste, Tabasco sauce, lemon zest and seasoning. Spoon the marinade over the salmon, then cover loosely and leave to marinate in the refrigerator for 30 minutes, turning the salmon or spooning the marinade occasionally over the salmon.

Heat a large wok, then add 2 tablespoons of the oil until almost smoking. Stir-fry the carrot for 2 minutes, then add the mangetout peas and stir-fry for a further 2 minutes. Add the oyster mushrooms and stir-fry for 4 minutes, until softened. Using a slotted spoon, transfer the vegetables to 4 warmed serving plates and keep warm.

Remove the salmon from the marinade, reserving both the salmon and marinade. Add the remaining oil to the wok, heat until almost smoking, then cook the salmon for 4–5 minutes, turning once during cooking, or until the fish is just flaking. Add the marinade and heat through for 1 minute. Serve immediately, with the salmon arranged on top of the vegetables and the marinade drizzled over.

Try This: FOR A LIGHTER OPTION: 86 FOR AN ALTERNATIVE: 114

Tuna & Mushroom Ragout

SERVES 4

225 g/8 oz basmati and wild rice
50 g/2 oz butter
1 tbsp olive oil
1 large onion, peeled and finely chopped
1 garlic clove, peeled and crushed
300 g/11 oz baby button mushrooms, wiped and halved
2 tbsp plain flour
400 g can chopped tomatoes
1 tbsp freshly chopped parsley
dash of Worcestershire sauce
400 g can tuna in oil, drained
salt and freshly ground black pepper
4 tbsp Parmesan cheese, grated
1 tbsp freshly shredded basil

To serve:
green salad
garlic bread

Cook the basmati and wild rice in a saucepan of boiling salted water for 20 minutes, then drain and return to the pan. Stir in half of the butter, cover the pan and leave to stand for 2 minutes until all of the butter has melted.

Heat the oil and the remaining butter in a frying pan and cook the onion for 1–2 minutes until soft. Add the garlic and mushrooms and continue to cook for a further 3 minutes.

Stir in the flour and cook for 1 minute, then add the tomatoes and bring the sauce to the boil. Add the parsley, Worcestershire sauce and tuna and simmer gently for 3 minutes. Season to taste with salt and freshly ground pepper.

Stir the rice well, then spoon onto 4 serving plates and top with the tuna and mushroom mixture. Sprinkle with a spoonful of grated Parmesan cheese and some shredded basil for each portion and serve immediately with a green salad and chunks of garlic bread.

Try This: FOR A LIGHTER OPTION: 38   FOR AN ALTERNATIVE: 116

Ratatouille Mackerel

SERVES 4

1 red pepper
1 tbsp olive oil
1 red onion, peeled
1 garlic clove, peeled and
   thinly sliced
2 courgettes, trimmed and

cut into thick slices
400 g can chopped tomatoes
sea salt and freshly ground
   black pepper
4 x 275 g/10 oz small
   mackerel, cleaned and

heads removed
spray of olive oil
lemon juice for drizzling
12 fresh basil leaves
couscous or rice mixed with
   chopped parsley, to serve

Preheat the oven to 190°C/375°F/Gas Mark 5. Cut the top off the red pepper, remove the seeds and membrane, then cut into chunks. Cut the red onion into thick wedges.

Heat the oil in a large pan and cook the onion and garlic for 5 minutes or until beginning to soften.

Add the pepper chunks and courgette slices and cook for a further 5 minutes.

Pour in the chopped tomatoes with their juice and cook for a further 5 minutes. Season to taste with salt and pepper and pour into an ovenproof dish.

Season the fish with salt and pepper and arrange on top of the vegetables. Spray with a little olive oil and lemon juice. Cover and cook in the preheated oven for 20 minutes.

Remove the cover, add the basil leaves and return to the oven for a further 5 minutes. Serve immediately with couscous or rice mixed with parsley.

Try This: FOR A LIGHTER OPTION: 62   FOR AN ALTERNATIVE: 216

Fragrant Thai
Swordfish with Peppers

SERVES 4

550 g/1¼ lb swordfish, cut
   into 5 cm/2 inch strips
2 tbsp vegetable oil
2 lemon grass stalks, peeled,
   bruised and cut into
   2.5 cm/1 inch pieces
2.5 cm/1 inch piece fresh
   root ginger, peeled and
   thinly sliced
4–5 shallots, peeled and
   thinly sliced
2–3 garlic cloves, peeled and
   thinly sliced
1 small red pepper,
   deseeded and thinly
   sliced
1 small yellow pepper,
   deseeded and thinly sliced
2 tbsp soy sauce
2 tbsp Chinese rice wine or
   dry sherry
1–2 tsp sugar
1 tsp sesame oil
1 tbsp Thai or Italian basil,
   shredded
salt and freshly ground
   black pepper
1 tbsp toasted sesame seeds

For the marinade:
1 tbsp soy sauce
1 tbsp Chinese rice wine or
   dry sherry
1 tbsp sesame oil
1 tbsp cornflour

Blend all the marinade ingredients together in a shallow, nonmetallic baking dish. Add the swordfish and spoon the marinade over the fish. Cover and leave to marinate in the refrigerator for at least 30 minutes. Using a slotted spatula or spoon, remove the swordfish from the marinade and drain briefly on absorbent kitchen paper. Heat a wok or large frying pan, add the oil and, when hot, add the swordfish and stir-fry for 2 minutes, or until it begins to brown. Remove the swordfish and drain on absorbent kitchen paper.

Add the lemon grass, ginger, shallots and garlic to the wok and stir-fry for 30 seconds. Add the peppers, soy sauce, Chinese rice wine or sherry and sugar and stir-fry for 3–4 minutes.

Return the swordfish to the wok and stir-fry gently for 1–2 minutes, or until heated through and coated with the sauce. If necessary, moisten the sauce with a little of the marinade or some water. Stir in the sesame oil and the basil and season to taste with salt and pepper. Tip into a warmed serving bowl, sprinkle with sesame seeds and serve immediately.

Try This: FOR A LIGHTER OPTION: 92   FOR AN ALTERNATIVE: 342

Chilli Monkfish Stir Fry

SERVES 4

350 g/12 oz pasta twists
550 g/1¼ lb monkfish,
   trimmed and cut
   into chunks
2 tbsp groundnut oil
1 green chilli, deseeded
   and cut into matchsticks

2 tbsp sesame seeds
pinch of cayenne pepper
sliced green chillies,
   to garnish

For the marinade:
1 garlic clove, peeled

and chopped
2 tbsp dark soy sauce
grated zest and juice of
   1 lime
1 tbsp sweet chilli sauce
4 tbsp olive oil

Bring a large saucepan of lightly salted water to the boil and add the pasta. Stir, bring back to the boil and cook at a rolling boil for 8 minutes, or until 'al dente'. Drain thoroughly and reserve.

For the marinade, mix together the sliced garlic, dark soy sauce, lime zest and juice, sweet chilli sauce and olive oil in a shallow dish, then add the monkfish chunks. Stir until all the monkfish is lightly coated in the marinade, then cover and leave in the refrigerator for at least 30 minutes, spooning the marinade over the fish occasionally.

Heat a wok, then add the oil and heat until almost smoking. Remove the monkfish from the marinade, scraping off as much marinade as possible, add to the wok and stir-fry for 3 minutes. Add the green chilli and sesame seeds and stir-fry the mixture for a further 1 minute.

Stir in the pasta and marinade and stir-fry for 1–2 minutes, or until piping hot. Sprinkle with cayenne pepper and garnish with sliced green chillies. Serve immediately.

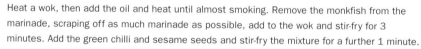

Try This: FOR A LIGHTER OPTION: 82   FOR AN ALTERNATIVE: 254

Chunky Halibut Casserole

SERVES 4

50 g/2 oz butter or margarine
2 large onions, peeled and sliced into rings
1 red pepper, deseeded and roughly chopped
450 g/1 lb potatoes, peeled
450 g/1 lb courgettes,

trimmed and thickly sliced
2 tbsp plain flour
1 tbsp paprika
2 tsp vegetable oil
300 ml/½ pint white wine
150 ml/¼ pint fish stock
400 g can chopped tomatoes
2 tbsp freshly chopped basil

salt and freshly ground black pepper
450 g/1 lb halibut fillet, skinned and cut into 2.5 cm/1 inch cubes
sprigs of fresh basil, to garnish
freshly cooked rice, to serve

Melt the butter or margarine in a large saucepan, add the onions and pepper and cook for 5 minutes, or until softened.

Cut the peeled potatoes into 2.5 cm/1 inch dice, rinse lightly and shake dry, then add them to the onions and pepper in the saucepan. Add the courgettes and cook, stirring frequently, for a further 2–3 minutes.

Sprinkle the flour, paprika and vegetable oil into the saucepan and cook, stirring continuously, for 1 minute. Pour in 150 ml/¼ pint of the wine, with all the stock and the chopped tomatoes, and bring to the boil.

Add the basil to the casserole, season to taste with salt and pepper and cover. Simmer for 15 minutes, then add the halibut and the remaining wine and simmer very gently for a further 5–7 minutes, or until the fish and vegetables are just tender. Garnish with basil sprigs and serve immediately with freshly cooked rice.

Try This: FOR A LIGHTER OPTION: 50 FOR AN ALTERNATIVE: 142

Mediterranean Fish Stew

SERVES 4

4 tbsp olive oil
1 onion, peeled and
   finely sliced
5 garlic cloves, peeled and
   finely sliced
1 fennel bulb, trimmed and
   finely chopped
3 celery sticks, trimmed and
   finely chopped

400 g can chopped tomatoes
   with Italian herbs
1 tbsp freshly chopped
   oregano
1 bay leaf
zest and juice of 1 orange
1 tsp saffron strands
750 ml/1¼ pints fish stock
3 tbsp dry vermouth

salt and freshly ground
   black pepper
225 g/8 oz thick
   haddock fillets
225 g/8 oz sea bass or
   bream fillets
225 g/8 oz raw tiger
   prawns, peeled
crusty bread, to serve

Heat the olive oil in a large saucepan. Add the onion, garlic, fennel and celery and cook over a low heat for 15 minutes, stirring frequently until the vegetables are soft and just beginning to turn brown.

Add the canned tomatoes with their juice, oregano, bay leaf, orange zest and juice with the saffron strands. Bring to the boil, then reduce the heat and simmer for 5 minutes. Add the fish stock, vermouth and season to taste with salt and pepper. Bring to the boil. Reduce the heat and simmer for 20 minutes.

Wipe or rinse the haddock and bass fillets and remove as many of the bones as possible. Place on a chopping board and cut into 5 cm/2 inch cubes. Add to the saucepan and cook for 3 minutes. Add the prawns and cook for a further 5 minutes. Adjust the seasoning to taste and serve with crusty bread.

Try This: FOR A LIGHTER OPTION: 42 FOR AN ALTERNATIVE: 148

Coconut Fish Curry

SERVES 4

2 tbsp sunflower oil
1 medium onion, peeled and
 very finely chopped
1 yellow pepper, deseeded
 and finely chopped
1 garlic clove, peeled
 and crushed
1 tbsp mild curry paste
2.5 cm/1 inch piece of root
 ginger, peeled and grated

1 red chilli, deseeded and
 finely chopped
400 ml can coconut milk
700 g/1½ lb firm white fish,
 e.g. monkfish fillets,
 skinned and cut into chunks
225 g/8 oz basmati rice
1 tbsp freshly chopped
 coriander
1 tbsp mango chutney

salt and freshly ground
 black pepper

To garnish:
lime wedges
fresh coriander sprigs

To serve:
Greek yoghurt
warm naan bread

Put 1 tablespoon of the oil into a large frying pan and cook the onion, pepper and garlic for 5 minutes, or until soft. Add the remaining oil, curry paste, ginger and chilli and cook for a further minute.

Pour in the coconut milk and bring to the boil, reduce the heat and simmer gently for 5 minutes, stirring occasionally. Add the monkfish to the pan and continue to simmer gently for 5–10 minutes, or until the fish is tender, but not overcooked.

Meanwhile, cook the rice in a saucepan of boiling salted water for 15 minutes, or until tender. Drain the rice thoroughly and turn out into a serving dish.

Stir the chopped coriander and chutney gently into the fish curry and season to taste with salt and pepper. Spoon the fish curry over the cooked rice, garnish with lime wedges and coriander sprigs and serve immediately with spoonfuls of Greek yoghurt and warm naan bread.

Try This: FOR A LIGHTER OPTION: 88   FOR AN ALTERNATIVE: 302

Crispy Prawn Stir Fry

SERVES 4

3 tbsp soy sauce
1 tsp cornflour
pinch of sugar
6 tbsp groundnut oil
450 g/1 lb raw shelled tiger
    prawns, halved
    lengthways

125 g/4 oz carrots, peeled
    and cut into matchsticks
2.5 cm/1 inch piece fresh
    root ginger, peeled and
    cut into matchsticks
125 g/4 oz mangetout peas,
    trimmed and shredded

125 g/4 oz asparagus spears,
    cut into short lengths
125 g/4 oz beansprouts
¼ head Chinese leaves,
    shredded
2 tsp sesame oil

Mix together the soy sauce, cornflour and sugar in a small bowl and reserve.

Heat a large wok, then add 3 tablespoons of the oil and heat until almost smoking. Add the prawns and stir-fry for 4 minutes, or until pink all over. Using a slotted spoon, transfer the prawns to a plate and keep warm in a low oven.

Add the remaining oil to the wok and when just smoking, add the carrots and ginger and stir-fry for 1 minute, or until slightly softened, then add the mangetout peas and stir-fry for a further 1 minute. Add the asparagus and stir-fry for 4 minutes, or until softened.

Add the beansprouts and Chinese leaves and stir-fry for 2 minutes, or until the leaves are slightly wilted. Pour in the soy sauce mixture and return the prawns to the wok. Stir-fry over a medium heat until piping hot, then add the sesame oil, give a final stir and serve immediately.

Try This: FOR A LIGHTER OPTION: 66   FOR AN ALTERNATIVE: 156

Stir–fried Tiger Prawns

SERVES 4

75 g/3 oz fine egg noodles
125 g/4 oz broccoli florets
125 g/4 oz baby sweetcorn,
  halved
3 tbsp soy sauce
1 tbsp lemon juice
pinch of sugar
1 tsp chilli sauce

1 tsp sesame oil
2 tbsp sunflower oil
450 g/1 lb raw tiger prawns,
  peeled, heads and tails
  removed, and deveined
2.5 cm/1 inch piece fresh
  root ginger, peeled and
  cut into sticks

1 garlic clove, peeled and
  chopped
1 red chilli, deseeded
  and sliced
2 medium eggs, lightly
  beaten
227 g can water chestnuts,
  drained and sliced

Place the noodles in a large bowl, cover with plenty of boiling water and leave to stand for 5 minutes, or according to packet directions; stir occasionally. Drain and reserve. Blanch the broccoli and sweetcorn in a saucepan of boiling salted water for 2 minutes, then drain and reserve.

Meanwhile, mix together the soy sauce, lemon juice, sugar, chilli sauce and sesame oil in a bowl and reserve.

Heat a large wok, then add the sunflower oil and heat until just smoking. Add the prawns and stir-fry for 2–3 minutes, or until pink on all sides. Using a slotted spoon, transfer the prawns to a plate and reserve. Add the ginger and stir-fry for 30 seconds. Add the garlic and chilli to the wok and cook for a further 30 seconds.

Add the noodles and stir-fry for 3 minutes, until the noodles are crisp. Stir in the prawns, vegetables, eggs and water chestnuts and stir-fry for a further 3 minutes, until the eggs are lightly cooked. Pour over the chilli sauce, stir lightly and serve immediately.

Try This: FOR A LIGHTER OPTION: 58   FOR AN ALTERNATIVE: 298

Red Prawn Curry with Jasmine–scented Rice

SERVES 4

½ tbsp coriander seeds
1 tsp cumin seeds
1 tsp black peppercorns
½ tsp salt
1–2 dried red chillies
2 shallots, peeled and chopped
3–4 garlic cloves
2.5 cm/1 inch piece fresh galangal or root ginger, peeled and chopped
1 kaffir lime leaf or 1 tsp

kaffir lime rind
½ tsp red chilli powder
½ tbsp shrimp paste
1–1½ lemon grass stalks, outer leaves removed and thinly sliced
750 ml/1¼ pints coconut milk
1 red chilli deseeded and thinly sliced
2 tbsp Thai fish sauce
2 tsp soft brown sugar
1 red pepper, deseeded and

thinly sliced
550 g/1¼ lb large peeled tiger prawns
2 fresh lime leaves, shredded (optional)
2 tbsp fresh mint leaves, shredded
2 tbsp Thai or Italian basil leaves, shredded
freshly cooked Thai fragrant rice, to serve

Using a pestle and mortar or a spice grinder, grind the coriander and cumin seeds, peppercorns and salt to a fine powder. Add the dried chillies one at a time and grind to a fine powder.

Place the shallots, garlic, galangal or ginger, kaffir lime leaf or rind, chilli powder and shrimp paste in a food processor. Add the ground spices and process until a thick paste forms. Scrape down the bowl once or twice, adding a few drops of water if the mixture is too thick and not forming a paste. Stir in the lemon grass.

Transfer the paste to a large wok and cook over a medium heat for 2–3 minutes or until fragrant.

Stir in the coconut milk, bring to the boil, then lower the heat and simmer for about 10 minutes. Add the chilli, fish sauce, sugar and red pepper and simmer for 15 minutes.

Stir in the prawns and cook for 5 minutes, or until the prawns are pink and tender. Stir in the shredded herbs, heat for a further minute and serve immediately with the cooked rice.

Try This: FOR A LIGHTER OPTION: 52   FOR AN ALTERNATIVE: 158

Lobster & Prawn Curry

SERVES 4

225 g/8 oz cooked lobster meat, shelled if necessary
225 g/8 oz raw tiger prawns, peeled and deveined
2 tbsp groundnut oil
2 bunches spring onions, trimmed and thickly sliced

2 garlic cloves, peeled and chopped
2.5 cm/1 inch piece fresh root ginger, peeled and cut into matchsticks
2 tbsp Thai red curry paste
grated zest and juice of 1 lime

200 ml/7 fl oz coconut cream
salt and freshly ground black pepper
3 tbsp freshly chopped coriander
freshly cooked Thai fragrant rice, to serve

Using a sharp knife, slice the lobster meat thickly. Wash the tiger prawns and pat dry with absorbent kitchen paper. Make a small 1 cm/½ inch cut at the tail end of each prawn and reserve.

Heat a large wok, then add the oil and, when hot, stir-fry the lobster and tiger prawns for 4–6 minutes, or until pink. Using a slotted spoon, transfer to a plate and keep warm in a low oven.

Add the spring onions and stir-fry for 2 minutes, then stir in the garlic and ginger and stir-fry for a further 2 minutes. Add the curry paste and stir-fry for 1 minute.

Pour in the coconut cream, lime zest and juice and the seasoning. Bring to the boil and simmer for 1 minute. Return the prawns and lobster and any juices to the wok and simmer for 2 minutes. Stir in two-thirds of the freshly chopped coriander to the wok mixture, then sprinkle with the remaining coriander and serve immediately.

Try This: FOR A LIGHTER OPTION: 84 FOR AN ALTERNATIVE: 320

Fruits de Mer Stir Fry

SERVES 4

450 g/1 lb mixed fresh
  shellfish, such as tiger
  prawns, squid, scallops
  and mussels
2.5 cm/1 inch piece fresh
  root ginger
2 garlic cloves, peeled
  and crushed

2 green chillies, deseeded
  and finely chopped
3 tbsp light soy sauce
2 tbsp olive oil
200 g/7 oz baby
  sweetcorn, rinsed
200 g/7 oz asparagus tips,
  trimmed and cut in half

200 g/7 oz mangetout,
  trimmed
2 tbsp plum sauce
4 spring onions, trimmed
  and shredded, to garnish
freshly cooked rice, to serve

Prepare the shellfish. Peel the prawns and if necessary remove the thin black veins from the back of the prawns. Lightly rinse the squid rings and clean the scallops if necessary. Remove and discard any mussels that are open. Scrub and debeard the remaining mussels, removing any barnacles from the shells. Cover the mussels with cold water until required.

Peel the root ginger and either coarsely grate or shred finely with a sharp knife and place into a small bowl. Add the garlic and chillies to the small bowl, pour in the soy sauce and mix well.

Place the mixed shellfish, except the mussels in a bowl and pour over the marinade. Stir, cover and leave for 15 minutes.

Heat a wok until hot, then add the oil and heat until almost smoking. Add the prepared vegetables, stir-fry for 3 minutes, then stir in the plum sauce.

Add the shellfish and the mussels with the marinade and stir-fry for a further 3–4 minutes, or until the fish is cooked. Discard any mussels that have not opened. Garnish with the spring onions and serve immediately with the freshly cooked rice.

Try This: FOR A LIGHTER OPTION: 50   FOR AN ALTERNATIVE: 148

Seafood Special

SERVES 4

2 tbsp olive oil 4 garlic
    cloves, peeled
125 g/4 oz squid, cut into rings
300 ml/½ pint medium-dry
    white wine
400 g can chopped tomatoes
2 tbsp fresh parsley,

finely chopped
225 g/8 oz live mussels,
    cleaned and beards
    removed
125 g/4 oz monkfish fillet
125 g/4 oz fresh tuna
4 slices of Italian bread

To garnish:
225 g/8 oz large, unpeeled
    prawns, cooked
4 langoustines, cooked
3 tbsp freshly
    chopped parsley

Heat the olive oil in a saucepan. Chop half of the garlic, add to the saucepan and gently cook for 1–2 minutes. Add the squid, 150 ml/¼ pint of the wine together with the tomatoes and simmer for 10–15 minutes.

Chop the remaining garlic and place with the remaining wine and 2 tablespoons of the parsley in another saucepan. Add the cleaned mussels to the pan, cover and cook for 7–8 minutes. Discard any mussels that have not opened, then remove the remaining mussels with a slotted spoon and add to the squid and tomato mixture. Reserve the liquor.

Cut the monkfish and tuna into chunks and place in the saucepan with the mussels' cooking liquor. Simmer for about 5 minutes, or until the fish is just tender.

Mix all the cooked fish and shellfish, with the exception of the prawns and langoustines, with the tomato mixture and cooking liquor in a large saucepan. Heat everything through until piping hot.

Toast the slices of bread and place in the base of a large, shallow serving dish.

Pour the fish mixture over the toasted bread and garnish with the prawns, langoustines and chopped parsley. Serve immediately.

Try This: FOR A LIGHTER OPTION: 72 FOR AN ALTERNATIVE: 122

Coconut Seafood

SERVES 4

2 tbsp groundnut oil
450 g/1 lb raw king
  prawns, peeled
2 bunches spring onions,
  trimmed and thickly
  sliced
1 garlic clove, peeled
  and chopped

2.5 cm/1 inch piece fresh
  root ginger, peeled and
  cut into matchsticks
125 g/4 oz fresh shiitake
  mushrooms, rinsed
  and halved
150 ml/¼ pint dry white wine
200 ml/7 fl oz carton

  coconut cream
4 tbsp freshly chopped
  coriander
salt and freshly ground
  black pepper
freshly cooked fragrant
  Thai rice

Heat a large wok, add the oil and heat until it is almost smoking, swirling the oil around the wok to coat the sides. Add the prawns and stir-fry over a high heat for 4–5 minutes, or until browned on all sides. Using a slotted spoon, transfer the prawns to a plate and keep warm in a low oven.

Add the spring onions, garlic and ginger to the wok and stir-fry for 1 minute. Add the mushrooms and stir-fry for a further 3 minutes. Using a slotted spoon, transfer the mushroom mixture to a plate and keep warm in a low oven.

Add the wine and coconut cream to the wok, bring to the boil and boil rapidly for 4 minutes, until reduced slightly.

Return the mushroom mixture and prawns to the wok, bring back to the boil, then simmer for 1 minute, stirring occasionally, until piping hot. Stir in the freshly chopped coriander and season to taste with salt and pepper. Serve immediately with the freshly cooked fragrant Thai rice.

Try This: FOR A LIGHTER OPTION: 56   FOR AN ALTERNATIVE: 176

Thai Curried Seafood

SERVES 4

2 tbsp vegetable oil
450 g/1 lb scallops, with
  coral attached if preferred,
  halved if large
1 onion, peeled and finely
  chopped
4 garlic cloves, peeled and
  finely chopped
5 cm/2 inch piece fresh
  root ginger, peeled and
  finely chopped
1–2 red chillies, deseeded

and thinly sliced
1–2 tbsp curry paste (hot or
  medium, to taste)
1 tsp ground coriander
1 tsp ground cumin
1 lemon grass stalk, bruised
225 g can chopped tomatoes
125 ml/4 fl oz chicken stock
  or water
450 ml/¾ pint coconut milk
12 live mussels, scrubbed
  and beards removed

450 g/1 lb cooked
  peeled prawns
225 g/8 oz frozen or canned
  crabmeat, drained
2 tbsp freshly chopped
  coriander
freshly shredded coconut,
  to garnish (optional)
freshly cooked rice or rice
  noodles, to serve

Heat a wok or large frying pan, add 1 tablespoon of the oil and when hot, add the scallops and stir-fry for 2 minutes or until opaque and firm. Transfer to a plate with any juices.

Heat the remaining oil. Add the onion, garlic, ginger and chillies and stir-fry for 1 minute or until they begin to soften.

Add the curry paste, coriander, cumin and lemon grass and stir-fry for 2 minutes. Add the tomatoes and stock, bring to the boil then simmer for 5 minutes or until reduced, stirring constantly. Stir in the coconut milk and simmer for 2 minutes.

Stir in the mussels, cover and simmer for 2 minutes or until they begin to open. Stir in the prawns, crabmeat and reserved scallops with any juices and cook for 2 minutes or until heated through. Discard the lemon grass and any unopened mussels. Stir in the chopped coriander. Tip into a large warmed serving dish and garnish with the coconut, if using. Serve immediately with rice or noodles.

Try This: FOR A LIGHTER OPTION: 82 FOR AN ALTERNATIVE: 100

Creamy Spicy Shellfish

SERVES 4

2 tbsp groundnut oil
1 onion, peeled and chopped
2.5 cm/1 inch piece fresh
    root ginger, peeled
    and grated
225 g/8 oz queen scallops,
    cleaned and rinsed
1 garlic clove, peeled

and chopped
2 tsp ground cumin
1 tsp paprika
1 tsp coriander seeds,
    crushed
3 tbsp lemon juice
2 tbsp sherry
300 ml/½ pint fish stock

150 ml/¼ pint double cream
225 g/8 oz peeled prawns
225 g/8 oz cooked
    mussels, shelled
salt and freshly ground
    black pepper
2 tbsp freshly chopped
    coriander

Heat a large wok, then add the oil and when hot, stir-fry the onion and ginger for 2 minutes, or until softened. Add the scallops and stir-fry for 2 minutes, or until the scallops are just cooked. Using a slotted spoon, carefully transfer the scallops to a bowl and keep warm in a low oven.

Stir in the garlic, ground cumin, paprika and crushed coriander seeds and cook for 1 minute, stirring constantly. Pour in the lemon juice, sherry and fish stock and bring to the boil. Boil rapidly until reduced by half and slightly thickened.

Stir in the cream and return the scallops and any scallop juices to the wok. Bring to the boil and simmer for 1 minute. Add the prawns and mussels and heat through until piping hot. Season to taste with salt and pepper. Sprinkle with freshly chopped coriander and serve immediately.

Try This: FOR A LIGHTER OPTION: 64   FOR AN ALTERNATIVE: 220

Thai Coconut Crab Curry

SERVES 4

1 onion
4 garlic cloves
5 cm/2 inch piece fresh
   root ginger
2 tbsp vegetable oil
2–3 tsp hot curry paste

400 g/14 oz coconut milk
2 large dressed crabs, white
   and dark meat separated
2 lemon grass stalks, peeled
   and bruised
6 spring onions, trimmed

   and chopped
2 tbsp freshly shredded Thai
   basil or mint, plus extra,
   to garnish
freshly boiled rice,
   to serve

Peel the onion and chop finely. Peel the garlic cloves, then either crush or finely chop. Peel the ginger and either grate coarsely or cut into very thin shreds. Reserve.

Heat a wok or large frying pan, add the oil and when hot, add the onion, garlic and ginger and stir-fry for 2 minutes, or until the onion is beginning to soften. Stir in the curry paste and stir-fry for 1 minute.

Stir the coconut milk into the vegetable mixture with the dark crabmeat. Add the lemon grass, then bring the mixture slowly to the boil, stirring frequently.

Add the spring onions and simmer gently for 15 minutes or until the sauce has thickened. Remove and discard the lemon grass stalks.

Add the white crabmeat and the shredded basil or mint and stir very gently for 1–2 minutes or until heated through and piping hot. Try to prevent the crabmeat from breaking up.

Spoon the curry over boiled rice on warmed individual plates, sprinkle with basil or mint leaves and serve immediately.

Try This: FOR A LIGHTER OPTION: 78   FOR AN ALTERNATIVE: 244

Mussels Arrabbiata

SERVES 4

1.8 kg/4 lb mussels
3–4 tbsp olive oil
1 large onion, peeled and sliced
4 garlic cloves, peeled and finely chopped

1 red chilli, deseeded and finely chopped
3 x 400 g cans chopped tomatoes
150 ml/¼ pint white wine
175 g/6 oz black olives,

pitted and halved
salt and freshly ground black pepper
2 tbsp freshly chopped parsley
warm crusty bread, to serve

Clean the mussels by scrubbing with a small, soft brush, removing the beard and any barnacles from the shells. Discard any mussels that are open or have damaged shells. Place in a large bowl and cover with cold water. Change the water frequently before cooking and leave in the refrigerator until required.

Heat the olive oil in a large saucepan and sweat the onion, garlic and chilli until soft, but not coloured. Add the tomatoes and bring to the boil, then simmer for 15 minutes.

Add the white wine to the tomato sauce, bring the sauce to the boil and add the mussels. Cover and carefully shake the pan. Cook the mussels for 5–7 minutes, or until the shells have opened.

Add the olives to the pan and cook uncovered for about 5 minutes to warm through. Season to taste with salt and pepper and sprinkle in the chopped parsley. Discard any mussels that have not opened and serve immediately with lots of warm crusty bread.

Try This: FOR A LIGHTER OPTION: 48 FOR AN ALTERNATIVE: 222

Mussels Cooked with Lager

SERVES 4

1.5 kg/3 lb 5 oz live mussels
450 ml/16 fl oz lager
2 onions, chopped
5 garlic cloves,
   chopped coarsely

1 fresh green chilli, such as
   jalapeño or serrano,
   deseeded and thinly sliced
175 g/6 oz fresh tomatoes,
   diced, or canned, chopped

2–3 tbsp chopped
   fresh coriander

Scrub the mussels under cold running water to remove any mud. Using a sharp knife, cut away the feathery 'beards' from the shells. Discard any open mussels that do not shut when tapped sharply with a knife. Rinse again in cold water.

Place the lager, onions, garlic, chilli and tomatoes in a heavy-based pan. Bring to the boil.

Add the mussels and cook, covered, over a medium-high heat for about 10 minutes until the shells open. Discard any mussels that do not open.

Ladle into individual bowls and serve sprinkled with fresh coriander.

Try This: FOR A LIGHTER OPTION: 84 FOR AN ALTERNATIVE: 178

Thai Green Fragrant Mussels

SERVES 4

2 kg/4½ lb fresh mussels
4 tbsp olive oil
2 garlic cloves, peeled and finely sliced
3 tbsp fresh root ginger, peeled and finely sliced
3 lemon grass stalks, outer leaves discarded and finely sliced
1–3 red or green chillies, deseeded and chopped
1 green pepper, deseeded and diced
5 spring onions, trimmed and finely sliced
3 tbsp freshly chopped coriander
1 tbsp sesame oil
juice of 3 limes
400 ml/14 fl oz coconut milk
warm crusty bread, to serve

Scrub the mussels under cold running water, removing any barnacles and beards. Discard any that have broken or damaged shells or are opened and do not close when tapped gently.

Heat a wok or large frying pan, add the oil and when hot, add the mussels. Shake gently and cook for 1 minute, then add the garlic, ginger, sliced lemon grass, chillies, green pepper, spring onions, 2 tablespoons of the chopped coriander and the sesame oil.

Stir-fry over a medium heat for 3–4 minutes, or until the mussels are cooked and have opened. Discard any mussels that remain unopened.

Pour the lime juice with the coconut milk into the wok and bring to the boil. Tip the mussels and the cooking liquor into warmed individual bowls. Sprinkle with the remaining chopped coriander and serve immediately with warm crusty bread.

Try This: FOR A LIGHTER OPTION: 56   FOR AN ALTERNATIVE: 304

Scallops with Black Bean Sauce

SERVES 4

700 g/1½ lb scallops, with
 their coral
2 tbsp vegetable oil
2–3 tbsp Chinese fermented
 black beans, rinsed,
 drained and coarsely
 chopped
2 garlic cloves, peeled and

finely chopped
4 cm/1½ inch piece fresh
 root ginger, peeled and
 finely chopped
4–5 spring onions, thinly
 sliced diagonally
2–3 tbsp soy sauce
1½ tbsp Chinese rice wine or

dry sherry
1–2 tsp sugar
1 tbsp fish stock or water
2–3 dashes hot
 pepper sauce
1 tbsp sesame oil
freshly cooked noodles,
 to serve

Pat the scallops dry with absorbent kitchen paper. Carefully separate the orange coral from the scallop. Peel off and discard the membrane and thickish opaque muscle that attaches the coral to the scallop. Cut any large scallops crossways in half, leave the corals whole.

Heat a wok or large frying pan, add the oil and when hot, add the white scallop meat and stir-fry for 2 minutes, or until just beginning to colour on the edges. Using a slotted spoon or spatula, transfer to a plate. Reserve.

Add the black beans, garlic and ginger and stir-fry for 1 minute. Add the spring onions, soy sauce, Chinese rice wine or sherry, sugar, fish stock or water, hot pepper sauce and the corals and stir until mixed.

Return the scallops and juices to the wok and stir-fry gently for 3 minutes, or until the scallops and corals are cooked through. Add a little more stock or water if necessary. Stir in the sesame oil and turn into a heated serving dish. Serve immediately with noodles.

Try This: FOR A LIGHTER OPTION: 92 FOR AN ALTERNATIVE: 282

Oriental Spicy Scallops

SERVES 4

12 fresh scallops, trimmed
12 rashers smoked streaky
   bacon, derinded
2 tbsp groundnut oil
1 red onion, peeled and cut
   into wedges
1 red pepper, deseeded

and sliced
1 yellow pepper, deseeded
   and sliced
2 garlic cloves, peeled
   and chopped
½ tsp garam masala
1 tbsp tomato paste

1 tbsp paprika
4 tbsp freshly chopped
   coriander

To serve:
freshly cooked noodles
Oriental-style salad

Remove the thin black thread from the scallops, rinse lightly and pat dry on absorbent kitchen paper. Wrap each scallop in a bacon rasher. Place on a baking sheet, cover and chill in the refrigerator for 30 minutes.

Meanwhile heat the wok, then add 1 tablespoon of the oil and stir-fry the onion for 3 minutes, or until almost softened. Add the peppers and stir-fry for 5 minutes, stirring occasionally, until browned. Using a slotted spoon, transfer the vegetables to a plate and reserve.

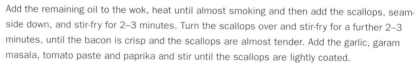

Add the remaining oil to the wok, heat until almost smoking and then add the scallops, seam-side down, and stir-fry for 2–3 minutes. Turn the scallops over and stir-fry for a further 2–3 minutes, until the bacon is crisp and the scallops are almost tender. Add the garlic, garam masala, tomato paste and paprika and stir until the scallops are lightly coated.

Stir in the remaining ingredients with the reserved vegetables. Stir-fry for a further 1–2 minutes or until the vegetables are piping hot. Serve immediately with noodles and an Oriental salad.

Try This: FOR A LIGHTER OPTION: 82   FOR AN ALTERNATIVE: 242

Ginger Lobster

SERVES 4

1 celery stalk, trimmed and
  finely chopped
1 onion, peeled and
  chopped
1 small leek, trimmed
  and chopped
10 black peppercorns
1 x 550 g/1¼ lb live lobster
25 g/1 oz butter
75 g/3 oz raw prawns,

peeled and finely chopped
6 tbsp fish stock
50 g/2 oz fresh root ginger,
  peeled and cut into
  matchsticks
2 shallots, peeled and finely
  chopped
4 shiitake mushrooms,
  wiped and finely chopped
1 tsp green peppercorns,

drained and crushed
2 tbsp oyster sauce
freshly ground black pepper
¼ tsp cornflour
sprigs of fresh coriander,
  to garnish
freshly cooked Thai rice and
  mixed shredded leek,
  celery, and red chilli,
  to serve

Place the celery, onion and leek in a large saucepan with the black peppercorns. Pour in 2 litres/3½ pints of hot water, bring to the boil and boil for 5 minutes, then immerse the lobster and boil for a further 8 minutes.

Remove the lobster. When cool enough to handle, sit it on its back. Using a sharp knife, halve the lobster neatly along its entire length. Remove and discard the intestinal vein from the tail, the stomach, (which lies near the head) and the inedible gills or dead man's fingers. Remove the meat from the shell and claws and cut into pieces.

Heat a wok or large frying pan, add the butter and, when melted, add the raw prawns and fish stock. Stir-fry for 3 minutes or until the prawns change colour. Add the ginger, shallots, mushrooms, green peppercorns and oyster sauce. Season to taste with black pepper. Stir in the lobster. Stir-fry for 2–3 minutes.

Blend the cornflour with 1 teaspoon of water to form a thick paste, stir into the wok and cook, stirring, until the sauce thickens. Place the lobster on a warmed serving platter and tip the sauce over. Garnish and serve immediately.

Try This: FOR A LIGHTER OPTION: 84 FOR AN ALTERNATIVE: 266

Stir-fried Squid with Asparagus

SERVES 4

450 g/1 lb squid, cleaned and cut into 1 cm/½ inch rings
225 g/8 oz fresh asparagus, sliced diagonally into 6.5 cm/2½ inch pieces
2 tbsp groundnut oil
2 garlic cloves, peeled and thinly sliced
2.5 cm/1 inch piece fresh root ginger, peeled and thinly sliced
225 g/8 oz pak choi, trimmed
75 ml/3 fl oz chicken stock
2 tbsp soy sauce
2 tbsp oyster sauce
1 tbsp Chinese rice wine or dry sherry
2 tsp cornflour, blended with 1 tbsp water
1 tbsp sesame oil
1 tbsp toasted sesame seeds
freshly cooked rice, to serve

Bring a medium saucepan of water to the boil over a high heat. Add the squid, return to the boil and cook for 30 seconds. Using a wide wok strainer or slotted spoon, transfer to a colander, drain and reserve.

Add the asparagus pieces to the boiling water and blanch for 2 minutes. Drain and reserve.

Heat a wok or large frying pan, add the groundnut oil and when hot, add the garlic and ginger and stir-fry for 30 seconds. Add the pak choi, stir-fry for 1–2 minutes, then pour in the stock and cook for 1 minute.

Blend the soy sauce, oyster sauce and Chinese rice wine or sherry in a bowl or jug, then pour into the wok. Add the reserved squid and asparagus to the wok and stir-fry for 1 minute. Stir the blended cornflour into the wok. Stir-fry for 1 minute, or until the sauce thickens and all the ingredients are well coated.

Stir in the sesame oil, give a final stir and turn into a warmed serving dish. Sprinkle with the toasted sesame seeds and serve immediately with freshly cooked rice.

Try This: FOR A LIGHTER OPTION: 88 FOR AN ALTERNATIVE: 164

Deep-fried, Pies & Pastry

Chinese Five–spice Marinated Salmon

SERVES 4

700 g/1½ lb skinless salmon
  fillet, cut into 2.5 cm/1
  inch strips
2 medium egg whites
1 tbsp cornflour
vegetable oil for frying
4 spring onions, cut
  diagonally into 5 cm/2

inch pieces
125 ml/4 fl oz fish stock
lime or lemon wedges,
  to garnish

For the marinade:
3 tbsp soy sauce
3 tbsp Chinese rice wine or

dry sherry
2 tsp sesame oil
1 tbsp soft brown sugar
1 tbsp lime or lemon juice
1 tsp Chinese five
  spice powder
2–3 dashes hot
  pepper sauce

Combine the marinade ingredients in a shallow, nonmetallic baking dish until well blended. Add the salmon strips and stir gently to coat. Leave to marinate in the refrigerator for 20–30 minutes.

Using a slotted spoon or fish slice, remove the salmon pieces, drain on absorbent kitchen paper and pat dry. Reserve the marinade.

Beat the egg whites with the cornflour to make a batter. Add the salmon strips and stir into the batter until coated completely.

Pour enough oil into a large wok to come 5 cm/2 inches up the side and place over a high heat. Working in 2 or 3 batches, add the salmon strips and cook for 1–2 minutes or until golden. Remove from the wok with a slotted spoon and drain on absorbent kitchen paper. Reserve.

Discard the hot oil and wipe the wok clean. Add the marinade, spring onions and stock to the wok. Bring to the boil and simmer for 1 minute. Add the salmon strips and stir-fry gently until coated in the sauce. Spoon into a warmed shallow serving dish, garnish with the lime or lemon wedges and serve immediately.

Try This: FOR A LIGHTER OPTION: 28 FOR AN ALTERNATIVE: 342

Luxury Fish Pasties

SERVES 4

For the quick flaky pastry:
250 g/8 oz butter
350 g/12 oz plain flour
2 pinches of salt

For the filling:
125 g/4 oz butter

125 g/4oz plain flour
300 ml/½ pint milk
225 g/8 oz salmon fillet,
   skinned, cut into chunks
1 tbsp freshly chopped
   parsley
1 tbsp freshly chopped dill

grated rind and juice of 1 lime
225 g/8 oz peeled prawns
salt and freshly ground
   black pepper
1 small egg, beaten
1 tsp sea salt
fresh salad leaves, to serve

Preheat the oven to 200°C/400°F/Gas Mark 6. To make the pastry, place the butter in the freezer for 30 minutes. Sift the flour and salt into a large bowl. Remove the butter from the freezer and grate coarsely, dipping the butter in the flour every now and again makes it easier to grate. Mix the butter into the flour, using a knife, making sure all the butter is coated thoroughly with flour. Add 2 tablespoons of cold water and continue to mix, bringing the mixture together. Use your hands to complete the mixing. Add a little more water if needed to leave a clean bowl. Place the pastry in a polythene bag and chill in the refrigerator for 30 minutes.

Place the butter in a saucepan and slowly heat until melted. Add the flour and cook, stirring for 1 minute. Remove from the heat and gradually add the milk a little at a time, stirring between each addition. Return to the heat and simmer, stirring continuously until thickened. Remove from the heat and add the salmon, parsley, dill, lime rind, lime juice, prawns and seasoning.

Roll out the pastry on a lightly floured surface and cut out 6 x 12.5 cm/5 inch circles and 6 x 15 cm/6 inch circles. Brush the edges of the smallest circle with the beaten egg and place two tablespoons of filling in the centre of each one. Place the larger circle over the filling and press the edges together to seal. Pinch the edge of the pastry between the forefinger and thumb to ensure a firm seal and decorative edge. Cut a slit in each parcel, brush with the beaten egg and sprinkle with sea salt. Transfer to a baking sheet and cook in the preheated oven for 20 minutes, or until golden brown. Serve immediately with some fresh green salad leaves.

Try This: FOR A LIGHTER OPTION: 88   FOR AN ALTERNATIVE: 334

Smoked Salmon Quiche

SERVES 6

225 g/8 oz plain flour
50 g/2 oz butter
50 g/2 oz white vegetable
  fat or lard
2 tsp sunflower oil
225 g/8 oz potato, peeled
  and diced

125 g/4 oz Gruyère cheese,
  grated
75 g/3 oz smoked salmon
  trimmings
5 medium eggs, beaten
300 ml/½ pint single cream
salt and freshly ground

black pepper
1 tbsp freshly chopped
  flat-leaf parsley

To serve:
mixed salad
baby new potatoes

Preheat the oven to 200°C/400°F/Gas Mark 6. Blend the flour, butter and white vegetable fat or lard together until it resembles fine breadcrumbs. Blend again, adding sufficient water to make a firm but pliable dough. Use the dough to line a 23 cm/9 inch flan dish or tin, then chill the pastry case in the refrigerator for 30 minutes. Bake blind with baking beans for 10 minutes.

Heat the oil in a small frying pan, add the diced potato and cook for 3–4 minutes until lightly browned. Reduce the heat and cook for 2–3 minutes, or until tender. Leave to cool.

Scatter the grated cheese evenly over the base of the pastry case, then arrange the cooled potato on top. Add the smoked salmon in an even layer.

Beat the eggs with the cream and season to taste with salt and pepper. Whisk in the parsley and pour the mixture carefully into the dish.

Reduce the oven to 180°C/350°F/Gas Mark 4 and bake for about 30–40 minutes, or until the filling is set and golden. Serve hot or cold with a mixed salad and baby new potatoes.

Try This: FOR A LIGHTER OPTION: 26   FOR AN ALTERNATIVE: 338

Trout with Cream Sauce

SERVES 4

550 g/1¼ lb rainbow
   trout fillets, cut
   into pieces
salt and freshly ground
   black pepper
2 tbsp plain white flour
1 tbsp finely chopped dill
groundnut oil for frying

For the cream sauce:
50 g/2 oz butter
2 bunches spring onions,
   trimmed and thickly sliced
1 garlic clove, peeled and
   finely chopped
300 ml/½ pint dry white wine
150 ml/¼ pint double cream

3 tomatoes, skinned,
   deseeded and cut
   into wedges
3 tbsp freshly chopped basil
freshly snipped basil,
   to garnish
freshly cooked, creamed
   herb potatoes, to serve

Remove as many of the tiny pin bones as possible from the trout fillets, rinse lightly and pat dry on absorbent kitchen paper. Season the flour and stir in the chopped dill, then use to coat the trout fillets.

Pour sufficient oil into a large wok to a depth of 2.5 cm/1 inch deep. Heat until hot and cook the trout in batches for about 3–4 minutes, turning occasionally, or until cooked. Using a slotted spoon, remove and drain on absorbent kitchen paper and keep warm. You may need to cook the trout in batches. Drain the wok and wipe clean.

Melt 25 g/1 oz of the butter in the wok, then stir-fry the spring onions and garlic for 2 minutes. Add the wine, bring to the boil and boil rapidly until reduced by half. Stir in the cream, with the tomatoes and basil, and bring to the boil. Simmer for 1 minute, then add seasoning to taste.

Add the trout to the sauce and heat through until piping hot. Garnish with freshly snipped basil and serve immediately on a bed of creamed herb potatoes.

Try This: FOR A LIGHTER OPTION: 74   FOR AN ALTERNATIVE: 348

Traditional Fish Pie

SERVES 4

450 g/1 lb cod or coley
  fillets, skinned
450 ml/¾ pint milk
1 small onion, peeled and
  quartered
salt and freshly ground
  black pepper

900 g/2 lb potatoes, peeled
  and cut into chunks
100 g/3½ oz butter
125 g/4 oz large prawns
2 large eggs, hard-boiled
  and quartered
198 g can sweetcorn,

  drained
2 tbsp freshly chopped
  parsley
3 tbsp plain flour
50 g/2 oz Cheddar cheese,
  grated

Preheat the oven to 200°C/400°F/Gas Mark 6, about 15 minutes before cooking. Place the fish in a shallow frying pan, pour over 300 ml/½ pint of the milk and add the onion. Season to taste with salt and pepper. Bring to the boil and simmer for 8–10 minutes until the fish is cooked. Remove the fish with a slotted spoon and place in a 1.4 litre/2½ pint baking dish. Strain the cooking liquid and reserve.

Boil the potatoes until soft, then mash with 40 g/1½ oz of the butter and 2–3 tablespoons of the remaining milk. Reserve.

Arrange the prawns and sliced eggs on top of the fish, then scatter over the sweetcorn and sprinkle with the parsley.

Melt the remaining butter in a saucepan, stir in the flour and cook gently for 1 minute, stirring. Whisk in the reserved cooking liquid and remaining milk. Cook for 2 minutes, or until thickened, then pour over the fish mixture and cool slightly.

Spread the mashed potato over the top of the pie and sprinkle over the grated cheese. Bake in the preheated oven for 30 minutes until golden. Serve immediately.

Try This: FOR A LIGHTER OPTION: 58 FOR AN ALTERNATIVE: 326

Russian Fish Pie

SERVES 4

450 g/1 lb orange roughy or haddock fillet
150 ml/¼ pint dry white wine
salt and freshly ground black pepper
75 g/3 oz butter or margarine
1 large onion, peeled and finely chopped
75 g/3 oz long-grain rice
1 tbsp freshly chopped dill
125 g/4 oz baby button mushrooms, quartered
125 g/4 oz peeled prawns, thawed if frozen
3 medium eggs, hard-boiled and chopped
550 g/1¼ lb ready-prepared puff pastry, thawed if frozen
1 small egg, beaten with a pinch of salt
assorted bitter salad leaves, to serve

Preheat the oven to 200°C/400°F/Gas Mark 6, 15 minutes before cooking. Place the fish in a shallow frying pan with the wine, 150 ml/¼ pint water and salt and pepper. Simmer for 8–10 minutes. Strain the fish, reserving the liquid, and when cool enough to handle, flake into a bowl.

Melt the butter or margarine in a saucepan and cook the onions for 2–3 minutes, then add the rice, reserved fish liquid and dill. Season lightly. Cover and simmer for 10 minutes, then stir in the mushrooms and cook for a further 10 minutes, or until all the liquid is absorbed. Mix the rice with the cooked fish, prawns and eggs. Leave to cool.

Roll half the pastry out on a lightly floured surface into a 23 x 30.5 cm/9 x 12 inch rectangle. Place on a dampened baking sheet and arrange the fish mixture on top, leaving a 1 cm/½ inch border. Brush the border with a little water.

Roll out the remaining pastry to a rectangle and use to cover the fish. Brush the edges lightly with a little of the beaten egg and press to seal. Roll out the pastry trimmings and use to decorate the top. Chill in the refrigerator for 30 minutes. Brush with the beaten egg and bake for 30 minutes, or until golden. Serve immediately with salad leaves.

Try This: FOR A LIGHTER OPTION: 26 FOR AN ALTERNATIVE: 332

Smoked Haddock Tart

SERVES 4

For the shortcut pastry:
150 g/5 oz plain flour
pinch of salt
25 g/1 oz lard or white
    vegetable fat, cut into
    small cubes
40 g/1½ oz butter or hard
    margarine, cut into
    small cubes

For the filling:
225 g/8 oz smoked haddock,
    skinned and cubed
2 large eggs, beaten
300 ml/½ pint double cream
1 tsp Dijon mustard
freshly ground black pepper
125 g/4 oz Gruyère
    cheese, grated

1 tbsp freshly
    snipped chives

To serve:
lemon wedges
tomato wedges
fresh green salad leaves

Preheat the oven to 190°C/375°F/Gas Mark 5. Sift the flour and salt into a large bowl. Add the fats and mix lightly. Using the fingertips rub into the flour until the mixture resembles breadcrumbs. Sprinkle 1 tablespoon of cold water into the mixture and with a knife, start bringing the dough together. (It may be necessary to use the hands for the final stage.) If the dough does not form a ball instantly, add a little more water. Put the pastry in a polythene bag and chill for at least 30 minutes.

On a lightly floured surface, roll out the pastry and use to line an 18 cm/7 inch lightly oiled quiche or flan tin. Prick the base all over with a fork and bake blind in the preheated oven for 15 minutes.

Carefully remove the pastry from the oven, brush with a little of the beaten egg. Return to the oven for a further 5 minutes, then place the fish in the pastry case.

For the filling, beat together the eggs and cream. Add the mustard, black pepper and cheese and pour over the fish. Sprinkle with the chives and bake for 35–40 minutes or until the filling is golden brown and set in the centre. Serve hot or cold with the lemon and tomato wedges and salad leaves.

Try This: FOR A LIGHTER OPTION: 50   FOR AN ALTERNATIVE: 346

Fish Puff Tart

SERVES 4

350 g/12 oz prepared puff
   pastry, thawed if frozen
150 g/5 oz smoked haddock
150 g/5 oz cod

1 tbsp pesto sauce
2 tomatoes, sliced
125 g/4 oz goats' cheese,
   sliced

1 medium egg, beaten
freshly chopped parsley,
   to garnish

Preheat the oven to 220°C/425°F/Gas Mark 7. On a lightly floured surface roll out the pastry into a 20.5 x 25.5 cm/8 x 10 inch rectangle.

Draw an 18 x 23 cm/7 x 9 inch rectangle in the centre of the pastry, to form a 2.5 cm/1 inch border. (Be careful not to cut through the pastry.) Lightly cut criss-cross patterns in the border of the pastry with a knife.

Place the fish on a chopping board and with a sharp knife skin the cod and smoked haddock. Cut into thin slices.

Spread the pesto evenly over the bottom of the pastry case with the back of a spoon.

Arrange the fish, tomatoes and cheese in the pastry case and brush the pastry with the beaten egg. Bake the tart in the preheated oven for 20–25 minutes, until the pastry is well risen, puffed and golden brown. Garnish with the chopped parsley and serve immediately.

Try This: FOR A LIGHTER OPTION: 62   FOR AN ALTERNATIVE: 330

Battered Cod & Chunky Chips

SERVES 4

15 g/½ oz fresh yeast
300 ml/½ pint beer
225 g/8 oz plain flour
1 tsp salt
700 g/1½ lb potatoes
450 ml/¾ pint groundnut oil

4 cod fillets, about 225 g/8 oz
    each, skinned and boned
2 tbsp seasoned plain flour

To garnish:
lemon wedges

sprigs of flat-leaf parsley

To serve:
tomato ketchup
vinegar

Dissolve the yeast with a little of the beer in a jug and mix to a paste. Pour in the remaining beer, whisking all the time until smooth. Place the flour and salt in a bowl, and gradually pour in the beer mixture, whisking continuously to make a thick smooth batter. Cover the bowl and allow the batter to stand at room temperature for 1 hour.

Peel the potatoes and cut into thick slices. Cut each slice lengthways to make chunky chips. Place them in a non-stick frying pan and heat, shaking the pan until all the moisture has evaporated. Turn them onto absorbent kitchen paper to dry off.

Heat the oil to 180°C/350°F, then fry the chips a few at a time for 4–5 minutes until crisp and golden. Drain on absorbent kitchen paper and keep warm.

Pat the cod fillets dry, then coat in the flour. Dip the floured fillets into the reserved batter. Fry for 2–3 minutes until cooked and crisp, then drain. Garnish with lemon wedges and parsley and serve immediately with the chips, tomato ketchup and vinegar.

Try This: FOR A LIGHTER OPTION: 90 FOR AN ALTERNATIVE: 344

Fried Fish with Thai Chilli Dipping Sauce

SERVES 4

1 large egg white
½ tsp curry powder or turmeric
3–4 tbsp cornflour
salt and freshly ground black pepper
4 plaice or sole fillets, about 225 g/8 oz each

300 ml/½ pint vegetable oil

For the dipping sauce:
2 red chillies, deseeded and thinly sliced
2 shallots, peeled and finely chopped
1 tbsp freshly squeezed lime juice
3 tbsp Thai fish sauce
1 tbsp freshly chopped coriander or Thai basil

To serve:
freshly cooked rice
mixed salad leaves

To make the dipping sauce, combine all the ingredients in a bowl. Leave for at least 15 minutes.

Beat the egg white until frothy and whisk into a shallow dish.

Stir the curry powder or turmeric into the cornflour in a bowl and season to taste with salt and pepper. Dip each fish fillet in the beaten egg white, dust lightly on both sides with the cornflour mixture and place on a wire rack.

Heat a wok or large frying pan, add the oil and heat to 180°C/350°F. Add 1 or 2 fillets and fry for 5 minutes, or until crisp and golden, turning once during cooking.

Using a slotted spatula, carefully remove the cooked fish and drain on absorbent kitchen paper. Keep warm while frying the remaining fillets.

Arrange the fillets on warmed individual plates and serve immediately with the dipping sauce, rice and salad.

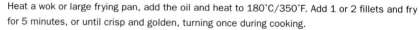

Try This: FOR A LIGHTER OPTION: 36   FOR AN ALTERNATIVE: 328

Goujons of Plaice
with Tartare Sauce

SERVES 4

75 g/3 oz fresh white
  breadcrumbs
3 tbsp freshly grated
  Parmesan cheese
salt and freshly ground black
  pepper
1 tbsp dried oregano
1 medium egg
450 g/1 lb plaice fillets

300 ml/½ pint vegetable oil
  for deep frying
fat chips, to serve

For the tartare sauce:
200 ml/7 fl oz prepared
  mayonnaise
50 g/2 oz gherkins, finely
  chopped

2 tbsp freshly snipped chives
1 garlic clove, peeled and
  crushed
2–3 tbsp capers, drained and
  chopped
pinch of cayenne pepper
sunflower oil for deep frying

Mix together the breadcrumbs, Parmesan cheese, seasoning and oregano on a large plate. Lightly beat the egg in a shallow dish. Then, using a sharp knife, cut the plaice fillets into thick strips. Coat the plaice strips in the beaten egg, allowing any excess to drip back into the dish, then dip the strips into the breadcrumbs until well coated. Place the goujons on a baking sheet, cover and chill in the refrigerator for 30 minutes.

Meanwhile, to make the tartare sauce, mix together the mayonnaise, gherkins, chives, garlic, capers and cayenne pepper. Stir, then season to taste with salt and pepper. Place in a bowl, cover loosely and store in the refrigerator until required.

Pour the oil into a large wok. Heat to 190˚C/375˚F, or until a small cube of bread turns golden and crisp in about 30 seconds. Cook the plaice goujons in batches for about 4 minutes, turning occasionally, until golden. Using a slotted spoon, remove and drain on absorbent kitchen paper. Serve immediately with the tartare sauce and chips.

Try This: FOR A LIGHTER OPTION: 72   FOR AN ALTERNATIVE: 336

Sweet-&-Sour Fish

SERVES 4

For the sweet-and-sour sauce:
2 tsp cornflour
300 ml/½ pint fish or chicken
  stock
4 cm/1½ inch piece fresh
  root ginger, peeled and
  finely sliced
2 tbsp soy sauce
2 tbsp rice wine vinegar or
  dry sherry
2 tbsp tomato ketchup or

tomato concentrate
2 tbsp Chinese rice vinegar
  or cider vinegar
1½ tbsp soft light
  brown sugar

125 g/4 oz carrot, peeled and
  cut into julienne strips
125 g/4 oz red or green pepper
125 g/4 oz mangetout, cut in
  half diagonally

125 g/4 oz frozen
  peas, thawed
2–3 spring onions, trimmed
  and sliced diagonally into
  5 cm/2 inch pieces
450 g/1 lb small thin skinless
  plaice fillets
1½–2 tbsp cornflour
vegetable oil for frying
sprigs of fresh coriander,
  to garnish

Make the sauce. Place the cornflour in a saucepan and gradually whisk in the stock. Stir in the remaining sauce ingredients and bring to the boil, stirring, until the sauce thickens. Simmer for 2 minutes, then remove from the heat and reserve.

Bring a saucepan of water to the boil. Add the carrot, return to the boil and cook for 3 minutes. Add the pepper and cook for 1 minute. Add the mange-tout and peas and cook for 30 seconds. Drain, rinse under cold running water and drain again, then add to the sweet and sour sauce with the spring onions.

Using a sharp knife, make crisscross slashes across the top of each fish fillet then lightly coat on both sides with the cornflour. Pour enough oil into a large wok to come 5 cm/2 inches up the side. Heat to 190°C/375°F, or until a cube of bread browns in 30 seconds. Fry the fish fillets, 2 at a time, for 3–5 minutes, or until crisp and golden, turning once. Using a fish slice, remove and drain on absorbent kitchen paper. Keep warm. Bring the sweet and sour sauce to the boil, stirring constantly. Arrange the fish fillets on a warmed platter and pour over the hot sauce. Garnish with sprigs of coriander and serve immediately.

Try This: FOR A LIGHTER OPTION: 46   FOR AN ALTERNATIVE: 340

Index